2

כָּל יִשְׂרָאֵל

The Prayers of Our People

By Gila Gevirtz

Activities:
Nina Woldin

D1440269

Editorial Committee:
Lauren Applebaum
Roberta Osser Baum
Rabbi Martin S. Cohen
Sarah Gluck
Ellen J. Rank
Pearl Tarnor

Behrman House, Inc.
www.behrmanhouse.com
www.kolyisrael.net

For Eve and Jonah; Jonathan, Brianna, Ethan, and Nate

— G.G.

The publisher gratefully acknowledges the cooperation of the following sources of photographs for this book: Stephen Coburn 91; Creative Image 25, 30; David E. Behrman 15, 19, Gila Gevirtz 8, 14, 22, 52; Michael Kaimowitz 69; Terry Kaye 85; Richard Lobell 6, 29, 65; Ginny Twersky 57

Book and cover design: Stacey May
Illustration: Pamela Hamilton (cover and story art), Daniel Griffo (activity art)
Project Editor: Terry S. Kaye

Contents

atya and Ben love to go to baseball games. They love wearing their home team's cap, doing the wave, and cheering when their favorite player hits a home run. At each game, the excitement builds from the very beginning as the stadium fills with thousands of fans. Everyone stands and sings the national anthem with pride and respect. It's the signal that the game is about to begin.

What is your favorite sport and team?

_____

How do you feel when everyone in a stadium rises and sings the anthem?

_____

Synagogue prayer services—from Tel Aviv to Tacoma—also begin in a certain way. The congregation rises, faces the Holy Ark, bows as a sign of respect to God, and recites a prayer called the בָּרְכוּ.

The בָּרְכוּ is like an announcement to the community: *The prayer service is beginning!*

Hi! I'm Minnie Minyan. Think about this: The words of the U.S. national anthem were written in 1814. The בָּרְכוּ was written almost *three thousand years ago* and has been recited since the time of the ancient Temple—בֵּית הַמִּקְדָּשׁ.

The prayer leader chants

בָּרְכוּ אֶת-יְיָ הַמְבֹרָךְ.

Praise Adonai, who is to be praised.

Then the congregation responds in agreement

בָּרוּךְ יְיָ הַמְבֹרָךְ לְעוֹלָם וָעֶד.

Praised is Adonai, who is to be praised forever and ever.

Our tradition teaches that a group of at least ten Jewish adults must be present in order to hold a community prayer service. That group is called a מִנְיָן.

Reading Rounds

The words below contain the family letters ב כ ך and ב ב. Read each line aloud.

1. **בכך** בָּרוּךְ כּוֹכָבִים אָכַל לָךְ כְּמַלְכֵּנוּ כָּמוֹךָ

2. **בב** בָּרְכוּ בִּדְבָרוֹ בַּלֵּבָב בְּבֵית אֲבָל הַמְבֹרָךְ

3. **בכ** מַכַּבִּי כָּל מְכַלְכֵּל מִכָּל בְּרָכוֹת בְּתוֹכֵנוּ

4. **בב** בָּחַר בּוֹרֵא בְּרָכָה בָּנוּ בָּרֵךְ אַבְרָהָם

5. **בכך** כָּמֹכָה יָדֶךָ בְּרוּכִים מֶלֶךְ יִמְלֹךְ

6. **בכ** כֵּן מִכָּל כְּמַלְכֵּנוּ כֶּלֶב בָּרְכוּ מְכַלְכֵּל

Prayer Words

Practice reading these words from the בָּרְכוּ.

bless! praise!	בָּרְכוּ
Adonai	יְיָ
who is to be blessed, praised	הַמְבֹרָךְ
blessed, praised	בָּרוּךְ
forever and ever	לְעוֹלָם וָעֶד

בְּרָכָה

Make the Connection

Draw a line to connect each Hebrew word to its English meaning.

forever and ever	הַמְבֹרָךְ
who is to be blessed, praised	בָּרְכוּ
blessed, praised	לְעוֹלָם וָעֶד
bless! praise!	יְיָ
Adonai	בָּרוּךְ

6

 **At the Root**

Most Hebrew words are built on **roots**. A root usually consists of three letters. Words with the root letters ברכ have **bless** or **praise** as part of their meaning. (*Reminder*: כ looks like this at the end of a word ך)

Read the words below, then draw a line from each word that is built on the root letters ברכ to the ברכ tree.

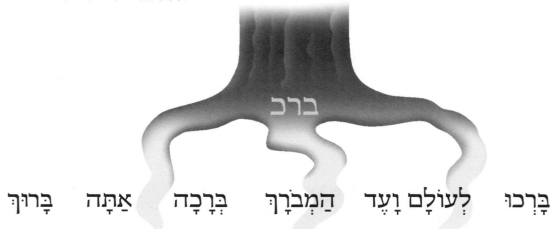

ברכ

בָּרְכוּ   לְעוֹלָם וָעֶד   הַמְבֹרָךְ   בְּרָכָה   אַתָּה   בָּרוּךְ

Now circle all the words in the בָּרְכוּ on page 5 that are built on the root ברכ.

 Did You Know? ··········

How did the בָּרְכוּ get its name? בָּרְכוּ is the first word of the prayer. The first word of a Hebrew prayer is often the name by which the prayer is known. Can you name another prayer that is known by its first word? Write it below in Hebrew or English.

_____

 The בָּרְכוּ does double duty. It's also part of the blessing that we recite before we read the Torah.

⚭ Language Link

Sometimes we use the word בָּרוּךְ to welcome others.

- We can greet a new member of our class, a friend, or a guest in our home by saying "בָּרוּךְ הַבָּא"—"Welcome!" (literally, "Praised is the one who comes").

- For a girl or a woman we say "בְּרוּכָה הַבָּאָה."

- If we are welcoming more than one person, we use the plural form בְּרוּכִים הַבָּאִים (all male or male and female) or בְּרוּכוֹת הַבָּאוֹת (female only).

Match each Hebrew greeting with its illustration.

בְּרוּכוֹת הַבָּאוֹת

בְּרוּכִים הַבָּאִים

בְּרוּכָה הַבָּאָה

בָּרוּךְ הַבָּא

בְּרוּכִים הַבָּאִים
לְיִשְׂרָאֵל

Putting It in ConTEXT

As far back as the Bible, Jews have praised God for the good in their lives. For example, the Bible teaches that God promised Solomon's father, King David, that Solomon would build the Temple. King Solomon praised God when construction of the Holy Temple was completed.

Read King Solomon's words from the Bible.

בָּרוּךְ יְיָ אֱלֹהֵי יִשְׂרָאֵל אֲשֶׁר דִּבֶּר בְּפִיו אֶת דָּוִד אָבִי וּבְיָדוֹ מִלֵּא...

Praised be Adonai, the God of Israel, who honored through deeds the promise made to my father, David... **(I Kings 8:15)**

Underline the Hebrew word above that is built on the root בְרַכ.

Circle King Solomon's father's name in Hebrew.

Draw a box around God's Hebrew name.

We Pray It But Can't Say It

Some names are difficult to pronounce. It is *impossible* to pronounce God's name. Why? Tradition teaches us that thousands of years ago, the *kohanim*—the Temple priests in ancient Jerusalem—knew how to pronounce God's name. After the Temple was destroyed, the priests no longer said God's name, and the correct pronunciation was lost. Today we are not sure how God's name was pronounced, so we say "Adonai." (Some people say "הַשֵׁם"—the Name.)

God's name is written in different ways but is always pronounced Adonai when we pray. In most siddurim it is written יְיָ. In other siddurim and in the Bible (תָּנַ״ךְ), it is written יְהֹוָה. In yet other Hebrew books God's name is written 'ה.

Write your name two different ways that would both be pronounced the same.

_____   _____

Read and

Practice reading the following sentences. Draw a circle around God's name wherever it appears.

1. בָּרְכוּ אֶת-יְיָ הַמְבֹרָךְ.

2. בָּרוּךְ יְיָ הַמְבֹרָךְ לְעוֹלָם וָעֶד.

3. מֵאֵין כָּמוֹךָ, יְהֹוָה, גָּדוֹל אַתָּה וְגָדוֹל שִׁמְךָ בִּגְבוּרָה.

4. כִּי לְךָ ה׳ הַגְּדֻלָּה וְהַגְּבוּרָה וְהַתִּפְאֶרֶת.

5. יְיָ צְבָאוֹת שְׁמוֹ.

6. גָּדוֹל ה׳ וּמְהֻלָּל מְאֹד, וְלִגְדֻלָּתוֹ אֵין חֵקֶר.

7. בָּרוּךְ יְיָ אֱלֹהֵי יִשְׂרָאֵל.

8. אֲנִי יְיָ אֱלֹהֵיכֶם.

10

A Circle of Friends

We enter the synagogue as individuals and as families. But when we recite the בָּרְכוּ in a minyan, we become a prayer community. In the circle below write your name and the names of nine other people you would like to see at services.

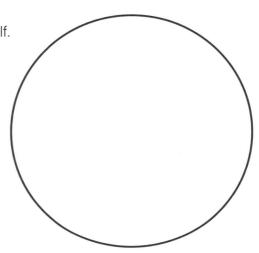

Describe one thing you like about being yourself.

_____

Describe one thing you like about being a member of your family.

_____

Describe one thing you like about being a member of your synagogue community.

_____

Write the words of the בָּרְכוּ in the correct order on the lines below.

אֶת יְיָ בָּרְכוּ הַמְבֹרָךְ
לְעוֹלָם בָּרוּךְ הַמְבֹרָךְ יְיָ וָעֶד

_____ .1

_____ .2

Which word in the בָּרְכוּ is also the first word of most blessings? _____

Use this clue to score bonus points in the "Carnival Duck!" game in Level 1—בָּרְכוּ—on your computer.

Ben and Batya were at a synagogue breakfast buffet. Ben took orange juice and a bagel. Batya chose cereal with strawberries and nuts. As they ate Ben said. "Trees and plants can't grow without light. That means that without light we couldn't have our favorite breakfast foods."

Which of your breakfast favorites are made from foods that grow on trees or plants?

_____

If there were no sunlight, it would also be hard to have picnics, play sports outside, and go to the beach.

What outdoor activities does daylight make it possible for you to enjoy?

_____

The Torah teaches us that God created the world and everything in it, and that God's first creation was light—אוֹר. Prayer helps us say thank you for these gifts. ▪▪

יוֹצֵר אוֹר

Off to a Good Start

The סִדּוּר is like a friend who reminds us of all the good in our lives. For example, the morning prayer service begins with יוֹצֵר אוֹר, blessings of thanks for the wonders of creation, including light—אוֹר— and darkness (we'll talk about darkness later in this chapter), and שָׁלוֹם. The יוֹצֵר אוֹר prayer is recited before the morning שְׁמַע. (You will learn about the שְׁמַע in the next chapter.)

> Jewish tradition teaches that God brought two kinds of אוֹר into our world—nature's light from the sun, moon, and stars, and the light of Torah's wisdom. Two ways people can add light are to perform acts of loving-kindness—גְּמִילוּת חֲסָדִים— and contribute to the שָׁלוֹם in our family and community. We show loving-kindness when we visit the sick and help feed those in need. We add peace to the world when we are patient with and respectful of others.

Practice reading יוֹצֵר אוֹר.

1. בָּרוּךְ אַתָּה, יְיָ אֱלֹהֵינוּ, מֶלֶךְ הָעוֹלָם,

2. יוֹצֵר אוֹר וּבוֹרֵא חשֶׁךְ, עֹשֶׂה שָׁלוֹם וּבוֹרֵא אֶת־הַכֹּל.

1. Praised are You, Adonai our God, Ruler of the world,
2. Who forms light and creates darkness, who makes peace and creates all things.

3. הַמֵּאִיר לָאָרֶץ וְלַדָּרִים עָלֶיהָ בְּרַחֲמִים,

4. וּבְטוּבוֹ מְחַדֵּשׁ בְּכָל יוֹם תָּמִיד מַעֲשֵׂה בְרֵאשִׁית.

5. מָה רַבּוּ מַעֲשֶׂיךָ, יְיָ,

6. כֻּלָּם בְּחָכְמָה עָשִׂיתָ, מָלְאָה הָאָרֶץ קִנְיָנֶךָ.

7. תִּתְבָּרַךְ, יְיָ אֱלֹהֵינוּ, עַל שֶׁבַח מַעֲשֵׂה יָדֶיךָ

8. וְעַל מְאוֹרֵי אוֹר שֶׁעָשִׂיתָ, יְפָאֲרוּךָ סֶלָה.

3. With mercy, You light the world and those who live in it.

4. In Your goodness, every day You renew creation.

5. How numerous are Your works, Adonai!

6. In wisdom, You made them all, the world is filled with Your creatures.

7. Be praised, Adonai our God, for the magnificent work of Your hands,

8. And for the light You created, may they glorify You.

9. אוֹר חָדָשׁ עַל צִיּוֹן תָּאִיר, וְנִזְכֶּה כֻלָּנוּ מְהֵרָה לְאוֹרוֹ.

9. Shine a new light on Zion, that we all may quickly be worthy of its glow.

10. בָּרוּךְ אַתָּה, יְיָ, יוֹצֵר הַמְּאוֹרוֹת.

10. Praised are You, Adonai, Creator of the heavenly lights.

 The words "every day You renew creation" remind us that every day the sun rises and gives us its light, new flowers bloom, and kittens are born. What are some other ways in which God renews creation?

מַעֲשֵׂה בְרֵאשִׁית

Prayer Words

Practice reading these words from יוֹצֵר אוֹר.

king, ruler	מֶלֶךְ
light	אוֹר
and creates	וּבוֹרֵא
darkness	חֹשֶׁךְ
Your hands	יָדֶיךָ
the heavenly lights	הַמְּאוֹרוֹת

Circle the word above that has the same root as אוֹר.

אוֹר וְחֹשֶׁךְ

 **Reading Rebus**

Read each line below. Write the correct Hebrew word next to each picture.

1. בָּרוּךְ אַתָּה, יְיָ אֱלֹהֵינוּ, _____ הָעוֹלָם

2. יוֹצֵר אוֹר וּבוֹרֵא _____

3. תִּתְבָּרַךְ, יְיָ אֱלֹהֵינוּ, עַל שֶׁבַח מַעֲשֵׂה _____

4. בָּרוּךְ אַתָּה, יְיָ, יוֹצֵר _____

Magnificent!

Read lines 5–8 of יוֹצֵר אוֹר in Hebrew and English (pages 13-14). If all God's creations are made "in wisdom" and are "magnificent," what does this prayer teach you about how you might behave toward other people?

_____

_____

 Reading Rounds

Read each line aloud.

1. הָעוֹלָם יוֹצֵר עֹשֶׂה עָלֶיהָ רוֹצֶה
2. מַעֲשֵׂה צִיוֹן צָרִיךְ שֶׁעָשִׂיתָ עַל
3. צָהֹב עָשִׂיתָ עוֹד צְרִיכָה עַכְשָׁו
4. מַעֲשֶׂיךָ צְדָקָה הַשְּׁבִיעִי וְעַל צֵאתְכֶם
5. לַצַּדִּיק עֶלְיוֹן עֲלֵיכֶם צִיצִית מִצְוָה

 Read and Repeat

Reread the lines above, this time with a partner. One person reads only words containing the letter עַ. The other person reads only words containing צ.

"Daylight is great but I also like the night," announced Ben as he and Batya waited for prayer services to begin. "Campfires and fireworks would be *b-o-r-i-n-g* without the night, and ghost stories wouldn't be nearly as scary."

"I guess you're right," said Batya. "I'd miss seeing the stars and the glow of Ḥanukkah candles in the dark—and I'd sure miss my sleep!"

What might you miss if night never came again and if the world were never dark?

_____

Just as **יוֹצֵר אוֹר** is recited before the morning **שְׁמַע**, so **מַעֲרִיב עֲרָבִים** is recited before the evening **שְׁמַע**.

Practice reading these lines from **מַעֲרִיב עֲרָבִים**.

1. בָּרוּךְ אַתָּה, יְיָ אֱלֹהֵינוּ, מֶלֶךְ הָעוֹלָם,

2. אֲשֶׁר בִּדְבָרוֹ מַעֲרִיב עֲרָבִים.

3. בְּחָכְמָה פּוֹתֵחַ שְׁעָרִים, וּבִתְבוּנָה מְשַׁנֶּה עִתִּים,

4. וּמַחֲלִיף אֶת הַזְּמַנִּים,

5. וּמְסַדֵּר אֶת הַכּוֹכָבִים בְּמִשְׁמְרוֹתֵיהֶם בָּרָקִיעַ כִּרְצוֹנוֹ.

6. בּוֹרֵא יוֹם וָלָיְלָה, גּוֹלֵל אוֹר מִפְּנֵי חֹשֶׁךְ, וְחֹשֶׁךְ מִפְּנֵי אוֹר,

7. וּמַעֲבִיר יוֹם וּמֵבִיא לָיְלָה, וּמַבְדִּיל בֵּין יוֹם וּבֵין לָיְלָה.

1. *Praised are You, Adonai our God, Ruler of the world,*

2. *whose word brings on the evening.*

3. *Who opens gates with wisdom, and with understanding alters time,*

4. *Who changes the seasons,*

5. *and arranges the stars in their heavenly order according to plan.*

6. *Creator of day and night, You roll light away from darkness and darkness from light,*

7. *Turning day into night and separating between day and night.*

‎8. יְיָ צְבָאוֹת שְׁמוֹ.

8. Adonai Tz'va'ot is God's name.

‎9. אֵל חַי וְקַיָּם, תָּמִיד יִמְלֹךְ עָלֵינוּ לְעוֹלָם וָעֶד.

‎10. בָּרוּךְ אַתָּה, יְיָ, הַמַּעֲרִיב עֲרָבִים.

9. May the living and eternal God rule over us always.

10. Praised are You, Adonai, who brings on the evening.

מַעֲרִיב עֲרָבִים and יוֹצֵר אוֹר are partner prayers that are like bookends to the Jewish day. יוֹצֵר אוֹר is said before the שְׁמַע in the morning and מַעֲרִיב עֲרָבִים is said before the שְׁמַע in the evening. Together, they remind us that God creates morning and night, light and darkness.

Read and **Circle**

Read the lines below. Then complete the activities that follow.

‎1. בָּרוּךְ עֹשֶׂה בְרֵאשִׁית

‎2. מֶלֶךְ מְהֻלָּל בַּתִּשְׁבָּחוֹת

‎3. וַאֲבָרְכָה שִׁמְךָ לְעוֹלָם וָעֶד

‎4. הוּא יְיָ אֱלֹהֵינוּ

‎5. תָּמִיד יִמְלֹךְ עָלֵינוּ לְעוֹלָם וָעֶד

Circle the two Hebrew words meaning "ruler" or "king" and "will rule."
Underline the two phrases meaning "always" or "forever and ever."

Prayer Words

Practice reading these words from the מַעֲרִיב עֲרָבִים prayer.

brings on the evening	מַעֲרִיב עֲרָבִים
the stars	הַכּוֹכָבִים
and night	וָלַיְלָה
living, lives	חַי
will rule	יִמְלֹךְ

P R A Y E R   P U Z Z L E

Complete the puzzle by writing the Hebrew word for each English word below.

Across

1. and night
5. brings on the evening

Down

2. the stars
3. will rule
4. living, lives

עֶרֶב

Putting It in ConTEXT

יוֹצֵר אוֹר and מַעֲרִיב עֲרָבִים are based on teachings from the first chapter of the first book of the Bible.

וַיֹּאמֶר אֱלֹהִים יְהִי-אוֹר וַיְהִי-אוֹר: ...וַיַּבְדֵּל אֱלֹהִים בֵּין הָאוֹר וּבֵין הַחֹשֶׁךְ: וַיִּקְרָא אֱלֹהִים לָאוֹר יוֹם וְלַחֹשֶׁךְ קָרָא לָיְלָה וַיְהִי-עֶרֶב וַיְהִי-בֹקֶר יוֹם אֶחָד:

God said, "Let there be light," and there was light...God separated the light from the darkness. God called the light Day, and the darkness God called Night. And there was evening and there was morning, Day One. **(Genesis 1:3–5)**

Next to the Torah scroll below, write the Hebrew word for *light* that appears in Genesis 1:3. Circle the Hebrew word for *light* and any variation of this word each time it appears in the יוֹצֵר אוֹר prayer on pages 13–14. How many words did you circle? _____

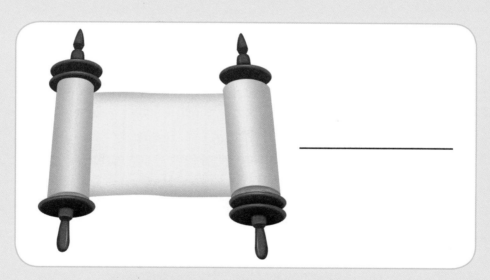

_____

Because the Torah says "And there was *evening* and there was *morning*, Day One," Jewish tradition teaches that each day begins in the evening. That is why, for example, Shabbat begins on Friday evening and ends on Saturday night when three stars can be seen in the evening sky.

A Loving Twosome

In the evening and morning prayer services, there are two blessings that come before the שְׁמַע. You have already learned the first of these two blessings.

Blessings before the שְׁמַע

	Theme	Evening Service	Morning Service
First blessing	Celebrates the wonder of creation and its renewal each day	מַעֲרִיב עֲרָבִים	יוֹצֵר אוֹר
Second blessing	Thanks God for giving us the Torah and mitzvot; our tradition teaches that these gifts show God's love for us	אַהֲבַת עוֹלָם	אַהֲבָה רַבָּה

 At the Root

מַעֲרִיב and עֲרָבִים are both built on the root ערב. Words built on the root ערב have **evening** or **mixed** as part of their meaning. Jewish tradition teaches that a tiny spark of God's light is mixed within the darkness.

Sometimes when we are worried or have a problem, it can feel as if we have a dark cloud over us. How might the teaching that even in darkness we can find a spark of God's light encourage us?

_____

To whom might you turn for help or support? Why? _____

_____

Language Link

It's easy to be friendly in Hebrew. You may already know that שָׁלוֹם means "peace," "hello," and "goodbye." But did you know that Israelis often say the word twice—שָׁלוֹם, שָׁלוֹם—to say hello?

עֶרֶב טוֹב means **good evening,** and לַיְלָה טוֹב means **good night.** When someone wishes you בֹּקֶר טוֹב, meaning **good morning,** a popular response is בֹּקֶר אוֹר, meaning **morning of light.** And on שַׁבָּת we greet everyone by saying, שַׁבָּת שָׁלוֹם, at any time—night *or* day.

Hebrew Howdy Do's

Draw a line to connect each greeting or phrase below to the picture that shows the time of day when it would be appropriate to say it. **Hint:** Two greetings can be connected to *both* pictures!

מַעֲרִיב עֲרָבִים      בֹּקֶר טוֹב

יוֹצֵר אוֹר   עֶרֶב טוֹב

שָׁלוֹם, שָׁלוֹם   שַׁבָּת שָׁלוֹם

לַיְלָה טוֹב   בֹּקֶר אוֹר

בֹּקֶר טוֹב

My Siddur

Practice each line below until you can read it with no mistakes. Then put a check in the box next to it.

☐	1. בָּרוּךְ אַתָּה, יְיָ, הַמַּעֲרִיב עֲרָבִים
☐	2. יוֹצֵר אוֹר וּבוֹרֵא חֹשֶׁךְ
☐	3. בְּחָכְמָה פּוֹתֵחַ שְׁעָרִים
☐	4. בְּמִשְׁמְרוֹתֵיהֶם בָּרָקִיעַ כִּרְצוֹנוֹ
☐	5. גּוֹלֵל אוֹר מִפְּנֵי חֹשֶׁךְ
☐	6. בָּרוּךְ אַתָּה, יְיָ, יוֹצֵר הַמְּאוֹרוֹת

Clue to Cyberspace

Draw a sun above the words below that have to do with day or light.
Draw a crescent moon above the words that have to do with night or darkness.

אוֹר חֹשֶׁךְ הַמֵּאִיר מְאוֹרֵי עֲרָבִים יוֹם בֹּקֶר

תָּאִיר לַיְלָה לְאוֹרוֹ הַמְּאוֹרוֹת הַכּוֹכָבִים עֶרֶב

Which *one* Hebrew word means the sun and the moon and stars? _____

Use this clue to score bonus points in the "Tile Tip" game in Level 2— יוֹצֵר/מַעֲרִיב —on your computer.

"Ben! Ben! You've got to hear this," shouted Batya as Ben entered the sanctuary with his religious school class.

Ben turned to look at Batya but before he could speak, she blurted out, "I've been chosen to lead my class in reciting מַעֲרִיב עֲרָבִים at synagogue services on עֶרֶב שַׁבָּת. I promised to practice until I can read it as well as I read English!"

Making a promise or pledge to others is a serious commitment. Keeping the promise or pledge lets others know they can count on you.

Describe a promise that you recently made to someone else.

_____

What was the most challenging part of keeping the promise? Why?

_____

How did it feel when you succeeded?

_____

The Jewish people believe that there is only one God. The שְׁמַע is the prayer in which we promise to be loyal to God. When we say the שְׁמַע, we try our best to concentrate and recite it with all our heart.

Our Pledge of Allegiance to God

Thousands of years ago, people believed that there were many gods. They believed that different gods ruled over different parts of nature—one over the sun, another over the moon, yet another over the sea.

The Bible teaches that there is only one God. Jewish tradition teaches that God rules over the world, loves שָׁלוֹם and צֶדֶק (justice), and cares about all people and all creation. The שְׁמַע is the Jewish people's pledge of allegiance to God.

The words of the שְׁמַע come from Deuteronomy, the fifth and final book of the Torah. They became part of our prayer service about two thousand years ago. Traditionally, many Jews say the שְׁמַע at least twice a day—during the morning *and* evening prayer services. Many also say it before going to bed at night and for strength when they are sad.

Practice reading the שְׁמַע.

שְׁמַע יִשְׂרָאֵל: יְיָ אֱלֹהֵינוּ, יְיָ אֶחָד.

Hear O Israel: Adonai is our God, Adonai is One.

The שְׁמַע can be recited standing or sitting. Some people recite it with their eyes closed or covered with their hand. This helps them concentrate on the prayer's words of faith and the pledge to be loyal to God.

שְׁמַע יִשְׂרָאֵל

Shh, Say It Softly, Please

In many congregations, the line immediately following the שְׁמַע is said quietly.

בָּרוּךְ שֵׁם כְּבוֹד מַלְכוּתוֹ לְעוֹלָם וָעֶד.

Blessed is the name of God's glorious kingdom forever and ever.

Unlike the words of the שְׁמַע itself, these words are not from the Bible. They were first recited in the Temple in ancient Jerusalem.

Practice reading these two lines aloud. Read the first line in a regular voice and the second line in a soft voice:

1. שְׁמַע יִשְׂרָאֵל: יְיָ אֱלֹהֵינוּ, יְיָ אֶחָד.

2. בָּרוּךְ שֵׁם כְּבוֹד מַלְכוּתוֹ לְעוֹלָם וָעֶד.

Why do we say the words following the שְׁמַע in a soft voice?

The ancient rabbis tell a midrash, a story based on the teachings of the Bible, to explain why. The midrash says that when our patriarch Jacob, also known as Israel, was dying, his sons said the words of the שְׁמַע to let their father know that they would be loyal to God. Jacob was so pleased that he responded, "Blessed is the name of God's glorious kingdom forever and ever." Because he was old and weak, he spoke the words very quietly. And now, so do we.

🔍 Word Sleuth

Draw a line to connect each word or phrase to its English meaning. Circle the Hebrew word for which no English meaning is listed.

forever and ever	מַלְכוּתוֹ
blessed	שֵׁם
God's kingdom	לְעוֹלָם וָעֶד
name	כְּבוֹד
_____	בָּרוּךְ

Now use the translation of the line following the שְׁמַע (at the top of this page) to discover the meaning of the new word. Write its meaning on the line above.

Prayer Words

Practice reading these words from the שְׁמַע.

hear	שְׁמַע
Israel	יִשְׂרָאֵל
our God	אֱלֹהֵינוּ
one	אֶחָד

Another Name

Write the English equivalent next to each Hebrew word. Then copy the numbered letters to find the missing name below.

___ ___ ___ ___ ___

1

___ ___ ___ ___ ___ ___

2   6

___ ___ ___   ___ ___ ___

3

___ ___ ___ ___

4

___ ___ ___

5

1. רִי
2. יִשְׂרָאֵל
3. אֱלֹהֵינוּ
4. שְׁמַע
5. אֶחָד

Another name for the Jewish people:

the Children of ___ ___ ___ ___ ___ ___
                  1   2   3   4   5   6

 **At the Root**

The word מַלְכוּתוֹ is built on the root מלכ. Words with the root מלכ have **king** or **ruler** as part of their meaning.

Read aloud the five words around the crown. Then circle the three root letters in each word.

כ   ל   מ

מַלְכֵּנוּ   מַלְכָּה

יִמְלֹךְ   מֶלֶךְ

מַלְכוּת

Which three letters appear in each word? (*Reminder*: בּ and ב are family letters and כ looks like this at the end of a word: ך) ____ ____ ____

 **Reading Rounds**

In lines 1–4 the dot for שׁ and שׂ identifies the letter *and* the vowel ◌ֹ. In lines 4-5, remember to read חַ at the end of each word as חַ◌.

1. עֹשֶׁר   קָדַשׁ   נְחֹשֶׁת   נָשָׂא   קָדָשִׁים

2. וְשִׁשָּׁן   עֲשׂוּהוּ   מֹשֶׁה   לִלְבֹּשׁ   חָשַׂף

3. שָׁלֹשׁ   לָשֹׂבַע   תְּטֹשׁ   וַיַּחְבֹּשׁ   עֹשֶׁק

4. שָׂמֵחַ   יֹשֶׁבֶת   שֹׁבֶר   וַיֶּחֱשֹׂף   חֹשֶׁךְ

5. הַמִּזְבֵּחַ   פּוֹתֵחַ   מִטְבֵּחַ   אוֹרֵחַ   לִשְׁבֵּחַ

28

Root Roundup

Read each line. Find and circle the words built on the roots listed in the first row of the chart. Some roots appear more than once. Check the chart to make sure that you find them all!

root	ברך	קדש	שלם	זכר	שמע	אכל	מלך	ערב
meaning	praise, bless	holy, set apart	wholeness	remember	hear	eat	rule, king	evening, mixed
# times root appears	3	1	1	2	2	1	3	2

1. אֲשֶׁר קִדְּשָׁנוּ בְּמִצְוֹתָיו

2. בָּרוּךְ אַתָּה יְיָ הַמַּעֲרִיב עֲרָבִים

3. שָׁלוֹם עֲלֵיכֶם מַלְאֲכֵי הַשָּׁרֵת

4. בָּרְכוּ אֶת-יְיָ הַמְבֹרָךְ

5. זִכָּרוֹן לְמַעֲשֵׂה בְרֵאשִׁית

6. מִמֶּלֶךְ מַלְכֵי הַמְּלָכִים

7. זֵכֶר לִיצִיאַת מִצְרַיִם

8. שְׁמַע יִשְׂרָאֵל יְיָ אֱלֹהֵינוּ

9. וְצִוָּנוּ עַל אֲכִילַת מָרוֹר

10. לִשְׁמֹעַ קוֹל שׁוֹפָר

לִשְׁמֹעַ קוֹל שׁוֹפָר

 **Language Link**

The phrase כְּלַל יִשְׂרָאֵל means **the entire Jewish people**. It includes every single Jew—Jews who like latkes and Jews who like pizza, Jews who live in Toronto and Jews who live in Jerusalem, Jews who play piano and Jews who play soccer. It tells us that we are one people, all of us, together.

As כְּלַל יִשְׂרָאֵל, we are taught to celebrate our many shared traditions, to be respectful of our differences, and to work together on behalf of our community. We attend worship services, organize coat drives for the poor, recycle newspapers, and conduct communal Passover seders.

Put a check mark next to the activities and places that help you feel like a member of כְּלַל יִשְׂרָאֵל.

_____ Shabbat prayer services _____ religious school _____ a trip to Israel

_____ a food drive _____ Purim carnival _____ High Holy Day services

_____ Jewish camp _____ Israel Independence Day celebration

_____ Other _____

כְּלַל יִשְׂרָאֵל

Putting It in ConTEXT

Let's look at the שְׁמַע again.

שְׁמַע יִשְׂרָאֵל: יְהֹוָה אֱלֹהֵינוּ, יְהֹוָה אֶחָד.

When we see the שְׁמַע in a Torah scroll (Deuteronomy 6:4), we notice that the last letter of the first word—ע—and the last letter of the last word—ד—are larger than the other letters. Together the two letters spell עֵד, meaning **witness**. This teaches that each of us can be a witness to God when we follow God's commandments. You are an עֵד to God when you perform mitzvot such as attending services, visiting the sick, and lighting Shabbat candles.

Write an example of how you witnessed God this week.

_____

Clue to Cyberspace

Look carefully at the strings of words below.

Find and circle the words that are part of the שְׁמַע.

1. הַמִּבְרָךְשְׁמַעלְיָלָהיִשְׂרָאֵליִיוֹםאֱלֹהֵינוּבָרְכוּיִיבְקֶראֶחָד

2. בָּרוּךְמֶלֶךְשֵׁםאֲשֶׁרכְּבוֹדמַלְכוּתוֹאֶתלְעוֹלָםלָאָרֶץצְרָיוֹצֶרָוָעֶד

Which word is also a number? _____

Use this clue to score bonus points in the "Balloon Float" game in Level 3—שְׁמַע—on your computer.

It was עֶרֶב שַׁבָּת. As Batya led her class in reciting מַעֲרִיב עֲרָבִים at synagogue services, her parents and grandparents beamed with pride.

When Batya or Ben has an important event—a concert performance, a tennis match, or a birthday—their family demonstrates their love by attending. Whenever Batya and Ben need help—solving a math problem, getting to piano lessons, or baking brownies—they can count on their family's love and support.

Describe one way that your family shows love for you.

_____

Describe something you do that shows love for your family.

_____

The וְאָהַבְתָּ reminds us to show love for God by following God's commandments. The וְאָהַבְתָּ comes right after the שְׁמַע in the סִדּוּר. The words of both prayers come from the Torah—chapter 6 in Deuteronomy.

> We affix a מְזוּזָה (plural מְזוּזוֹת)—a small case containing a tiny scroll with the שְׁמַע and the וְאָהַבְתָּ—on the doorposts of our house. It reminds us to observe God's מִצְווֹת.

Name two ways you can show love and respect for both God and other people. For example, you can give food to the needy.

1. _____

2. _____

Practice reading the וְאָהַבְתָּ.

1. וְאָהַבְתָּ אֵת יְיָ אֱלֹהֶיךָ

2. בְּכָל-לְבָבְךָ וּבְכָל-נַפְשְׁךָ וּבְכָל-מְאֹדֶךָ.

3. וְהָיוּ הַדְּבָרִים הָאֵלֶּה, אֲשֶׁר אָנֹכִי מְצַוְּךָ הַיּוֹם, עַל-לְבָבֶךָ.

4. וְשִׁנַּנְתָּם לְבָנֶיךָ, וְדִבַּרְתָּ בָּם בְּשִׁבְתְּךָ בְּבֵיתֶךָ,

5. וּבְלֶכְתְּךָ בַדֶּרֶךְ, וּבְשָׁכְבְּךָ וּבְקוּמֶךָ.

6. וּקְשַׁרְתָּם לְאוֹת עַל-יָדֶךָ, וְהָיוּ לְטֹטָפֹת בֵּין עֵינֶיךָ.

7. וּכְתַבְתָּם עַל-מְזֻזוֹת בֵּיתֶךָ וּבִשְׁעָרֶיךָ.

1. *You shall love Adonai, your God,*

2. *with all your heart, and with all your soul, and with all your might.*

3. *Set these words, which I command you this day, upon your heart.*

4. *Teach them to your children, and speak of them when you are at home,*

5. *and when you go on your way, and when you lie down, and when you get up.*

6. *Bind them as a sign upon your hand and let them be symbols between your eyes.*

7. *Write them on the doorposts of your house and on your gates.*

Our tradition teaches that we are commanded to love *and* to take the actions that demonstrate love. So, each מִצְוָה we do brings us closer to God and makes us more loving people.

Which מִצְוָה makes you feel closer to God or like a more loving person? Why?

_____

_____

33

I Can Learn!

Describe something you learned recently in a religious school class.

_____

The וְאָהַבְתָּ not only teaches us to love God but also to love Jewish learning—**Talmud Torah**, תַּלְמוּד תּוֹרָה. Reread lines 3–7 of the וְאָהַבְתָּ in Hebrew and in English on page 33. Circle the Hebrew word that refers to the cases we affix to our doorposts. (**Hint:** They contain a scroll with the שְׁמַע and וְאָהַבְתָּ.)

What do you most want to learn about Judaism? Why?

_____

_____

How can תַּלְמוּד תּוֹרָה help you become the person you want to grow up to be?

_____

_____

The Talmud teaches that תַּלְמוּד תּוֹרָה is equal to all the other מִצְווֹת:

$$\text{תַּלְמוּד תּוֹרָה כְּנֶגֶד כֻּלָּם.}$$

The study of Torah is equal to all [the mitzvot].

Why is תַּלְמוּד תּוֹרָה so important? One explanation is that studying תּוֹרָה helps us learn the other מִצְווֹת so that we can *do* them. Both the שְׁמַע and וְאָהַבְתָּ are teachings from the Torah. So, when you say them you are doing two מִצְווֹת—praying *and* תַּלְמוּד תּוֹרָה!

Jewish tradition teaches us to study תּוֹרָה with other Jews. Why do you think we are encouraged to study תּוֹרָה in community with others? What might you learn from others? What might you teach?

Prayer Words

Practice reading these words from the וְאָהַבְתָּ.

you shall love	וְאָהַבְתָּ
your heart	לְבָבְךָ
your soul	נַפְשְׁךָ
mezuzot	מְזֻזוֹת
your house	בֵּיתֶךָ

Missing Link

Complete each prayer phrase with the missing Hebrew word.

1. _____ (you shall love) אֵת יְיָ אֱלֹהֶיךָ

2. בְּכָל _____ (your heart)

3. וּבְכָל _____ (your soul)

4. וּכְתַבְתָּם עַל _____ (mezuzot)

5. _____ (your house) וּבִשְׁעָרֶיךָ.

Remember and Do!

After reciting the וְאָהַבְתָּ some congregations add these verses from
the Torah (Numbers 15:40–41).

1. לְמַעַן תִּזְכְּרוּ וַעֲשִׂיתֶם אֶת־כָּל־מִצְוֹתָי

2. וִהְיִיתֶם קְדֹשִׁים לֵאלֹהֵיכֶם.

3. אֲנִי יְיָ אֱלֹהֵיכֶם אֲשֶׁר הוֹצֵאתִי אֶתְכֶם מֵאֶרֶץ מִצְרַיִם

4. לִהְיוֹת לָכֶם לֵאלֹהִים. אֲנִי יְיָ אֱלֹהֵיכֶם.

1. That you will remember and do all my commandments
2. and be holy to your God.
3. I am Adonai your God who brought you out of the land of Egypt
4. to be your God. I am Adonai your God.

At the Root

The theme of the וְאָהַבְתָּ is our love for God. Below are the names of three prayers that speak of the love between God and the Jewish people. Can you find the root letters that are the same in each name?

Write the letters here. _____ _____ _____

וְאָהַבְתָּ   אַהֲבַת עוֹלָם   אַהֲבָה רַבָּה

Words built on the root **אהב** have **love** as part of their meaning.

Draw a heart around the three Hebrew words below that are built on the root **אהב**. Then circle their three root letters.

אַהֲבָה   אָבוֹת   אָהַבְתָּ   אַבְרָהָם   וְאָהַבְתָּ

Bonus: Underline the name of the person in the Torah who was the first Jew.

Root Match

Connect the root in the middle column to its matching Hebrew word on the right and the English meaning on the left.

English	Root	Hebrew
remember	אהב	זִכָּרוֹן
eat	מלכ	לִשְׁמֹעַ
hear	אכל	וְאָהַבְתָּ
love	שמע	אֲכִילַת
rule	זכר	מַלְכוּת

Putting It in ConTEXT

Jewish tradition teaches that the love between God and the Jewish people is so great that it is as if they married each other at Mount Sinai. God was the groom, the Jewish people the bride, and the Torah the marriage contract, or *ketubah*. The Song of Songs, a scroll in the Bible thought to have been written by King Solomon, tells the love story between God and the Jewish people. It teaches that God spoke to us, saying:

... הַשְׁמִיעִינִי אֶת־קוֹלֵךְ

כִּי־קוֹלֵךְ עָרֵב וּמַרְאֵיךְ נָאוֶה.

... Let me hear your voice

For your voice is sweet and your image is beautiful (Song of Songs 2:14).

List three qualities you admire in people you love.

1. _____   2. _____   3. _____

Why did you choose those qualities? _____

_____

Take Action

Turn to page 33 and read the וְאָהַבְתָּ in both Hebrew and English. Look for the ways we are told we can show our love for God. Copy the one that means the most to you. Explain your choice.

_____

_____

_____

Yours Truly

The word בֵּיתְךָ means "your house." It is made up of two parts:

בַּיִת   means "house."

ךָ   is an ending that means "you" or "your."

Many words in the וְאָהַבְתָּ end with ךָ.

Read the first three lines of the וְאָהַבְתָּ below and circle each word with the ending ךָ.

1. וְאָהַבְתָּ אֵת יְיָ אֱלֹהֶיךָ

2. בְּכָל־לְבָבְךָ וּבְכָל־נַפְשְׁךָ וּבְכָל־מְאֹדֶךָ.

3. וְהָיוּ הַדְּבָרִים הָאֵלֶּה, אֲשֶׁר אָנֹכִי מְצַוְּךָ הַיּוֹם, עַל־לְבָבֶךָ.

How many words did you circle? _____

What does the ending ךָ mean? _____ _____

Whom is the prayer addressing? _____

Language Link

The word בַּיִת describes many kinds of buildings. Read the Hebrew phrases below. Then, using the English clue, match each Hebrew phrase to its appropriate picture.

Where prayer services are held   בֵּית־כְּנֶסֶת

Where teachers work   בֵּית־סֵפֶר

Home of the U.S. President   הַבַּיִת הַלָּבָן

Where doctors work   בֵּית־חוֹלִים

Siddur Challenge

Write the number of each Hebrew word next to the matching English word. You will have four Hebrew words left. Put those remaining words in order to form a siddur phrase.

5. הַכּוֹכָבִים   4. חֹשֶׁךְ   3. אֶת   2. מֶלֶךְ   1. הַמְבֹרָךְ

10. אֶחָד   9. בָּרְכוּ   8. בֵּיתֶךָ   7. וְאָהַבְתָּ   6. יְיָ

_____ ruler, king   _____ you shall love   _____ darkness

_____ your house   _____ the stars   _____ one

_____ _____ _____ _____ ⬅

Write the name of the prayer in which you will find this phrase. _____

Clue to Cyberspace

Our tradition teaches that our actions can bring us closer to God. Look back at the English translation of the וְאָהַבְתָּ on page 33. Then circle each "action" word below.

1. וְאָהַבְתָּ אֵת יְיָ אֱלֹהֶיךָ
2. וְשִׁנַּנְתָּם לְבָנֶיךָ, וְדִבַּרְתָּ בָּם בְּשִׁבְתְּךָ בְּבֵיתֶךָ
3. וּבְלֶכְתְּךָ בַדֶּרֶךְ, וּבְשָׁכְבְּךָ וּבְקוּמֶךָ
4. וּקְשַׁרְתָּם לְאוֹת עַל-יָדֶךָ
5. וּכְתַבְתָּם עַל-מְזֻזוֹת בֵּיתֶךָ

Which word in line 5 above means "your house"? _____

Use this clue to score bonus points in the "Carnival Duck!" game in Level 4— וְאָהַבְתָּ —on your computer.

On Sunday Ben and Batya rode their bikes to religious school. While racing downhill, Ben's front wheel brushed against Batya's back wheel. In a flash, Ben short stopped, did a hand spring off the handle bars, then landed on his feet. "It was awesome. Not a scratch on me—*a miracle!*" he told friends.

Describe something that has happened to you that seemed like a miracle.

_____

_____

How did you feel? Why? _____

The Bible teaches that God freed the Israelites from slavery in Egypt and parted the Sea of Reeds so that they could cross to safety. The parting of the waters was a miracle to the Israelites. In gratitude, they sang a song of praise to God. They sang מִי כָמֹכָה, "Who is like You?" Today we express gratitude for our freedom by reciting the מִי כָמֹכָה prayer.

Practice reading the מִי כָמֹכָה.

1. מִי־כָמֹכָה בָּאֵלִם, יְיָ?

2. מִי כָּמֹכָה, נֶאְדָּר בַּקֹּדֶשׁ,

3. נוֹרָא תְהִלֹּת, עֹשֵׂה פֶלֶא?

1. *Who is like You among the gods [that other nations worship], Adonai?*

2. *Who is like You, majestic in holiness,*

3. *Awesome in splendor, doing wonders?*

Practice reading these two additional verses of the מִי כָמֹכָה that we read in the morning service.

4. שִׁירָה חֲדָשָׁה שִׁבְּחוּ גְאוּלִים לְשִׁמְךָ עַל שְׂפַת הַיָּם.

5. יַחַד כֻּלָּם הוֹדוּ וְהִמְלִיכוּ, וְאָמְרוּ,

6. יְיָ יִמְלֹךְ לְעוֹלָם וָעֶד.

4. *At the shore of the sea, the redeemed [Israelites] sang a new song of praise for You.*

5. *Together they acclaimed Your sovereignty, saying,*

6. *"Adonai will rule forever."*

7. צוּר יִשְׂרָאֵל, קוּמָה בְּעֶזְרַת יִשְׂרָאֵל.

8. וּפְדֵה כִנְאֻמֶךָ יְהוּדָה וְיִשְׂרָאֵל.

9. גֹּאֲלֵנוּ, יְיָ צְבָאוֹת שְׁמוֹ, קְדוֹשׁ יִשְׂרָאֵל.

10. בָּרוּךְ אַתָּה, יְיָ, גָּאַל יִשְׂרָאֵל.

7. *Rock of Israel, rise to the defense of Israel.*

8. *Keep your promise to redeem Judah and Israel.*

9. *Our Redeemer, Adonai Tz'va'ot is Your name, the Holy One of Israel.*

10. *Praised are You, Adonai, Redeemer of Israel.*

The Mitzvah of פִּדְיוֹן שְׁבוּיִים

Our tradition teaches that, as we were freed from slavery in Egypt, so we must help free others. We call this mitzvah פִּדְיוֹן שְׁבוּיִים (Redeeming Captives).

It is not easy to free people who are oppressed. So we must work with others in our community to perform the mitzvah of פִּדְיוֹן שְׁבוּיִים. Together we can collect צְדָקָה, contact politicians, and participate in demonstrations to help those who suffer. Name something you can do to help people who suffer.

Prayer Words

Practice reading these words from the מִי כָמֹכָה prayer.

who is like You	מִי כָמֹכָה
among the gods (that other nations worship)	בָּאֵלִם
in holiness	בַּקֹּדֶשׁ
splendor, praises	תְהִלֹּת
wonder(s)	פֶּלֶא

Word Search

Find and circle the five Hebrew words in the grid below. Look across and down.
Then write the English meaning below each Hebrew word.

מִי כָמֹכָה   תְהִלֹּת   בָּאֵלִם   פֶּלֶא   בַּקֹּדֶשׁ

_____ _____ _____ _____ _____

מ	ס	ל	א	ב	ת
י	ב	ל	פ	ה	ה
כ	צ	ת	שׁ	ט	ל
מ	ה	ק	ד	ר	ת
כ	ט	ח	ג	ע	ר
ה	ס	שׁ	ד	ק	ב

Putting It in ConTEXT

Below is a page from chapter 15 in the Book of Exodus. It is part of the song the Israelites sang after crossing the Sea of Reeds. The Torah says that the waters formed a wall to the right and left and the Israelites crossed on dry land. In the Torah the words of the song are laid out to look like a brick wall.

Be a detective: Find and read the twelve words of the מִי כָמֹכָה below.

Be a super detective: Find and read the verse that has the Hebrew words for "Adonai" and "will rule" and the Hebrew phrase for "forever and ever."

אָמַר 9
אֹיֵב אֶרְדֹּף אַשִּׂיג   אֲחַלֵּק שָׁלָל תִּמְלָאֵמוֹ
נַפְשִׁי   אָרִיק חַרְבִּי תּוֹרִישֵׁמוֹ יָדִי: נָשַׁפְתָּ י
בְרוּחֲךָ כִּסָּמוֹ יָם   צָלֲלוּ כַּעוֹפֶרֶת בְּמַיִם
אַדִּירִים 11   מִי־כָמֹכָה בָּאֵלִם יְהֹוָה   מִי
כָמֹכָה נֶאְדָּר בַּקֹּדֶשׁ   נוֹרָא תְהִלֹּת עֹשֵׂה־
פֶלֶא: 12   נָטִיתָ יְמִינְךָ תִּבְלָעֵמוֹ אָרֶץ: נָחִיתָ
13
בְחַסְדְּךָ עַם־זוּ גָּאָלְתָּ   נֵהַלְתָּ בְעָזְּךָ אֶל־נְוֵה
קָדְשֶׁךָ: 14   שָׁמְעוּ עַמִּים יִרְגָּזוּן   חִיל
אָחַז יֹשְׁבֵי פְּלָשֶׁת: אָז נִבְהֲלוּ אַלּוּפֵי טו
אֱדוֹם   אֵילֵי מוֹאָב יֹאחֲזֵמוֹ רָעַד   נָמֹגוּ
כֹּל יֹשְׁבֵי כְנָעַן: 16   תִּפֹּל עֲלֵיהֶם אֵימָתָה
וָפַחַד   בִּגְדֹל זְרוֹעֲךָ יִדְּמוּ כָּאָבֶן   עַד־
יַעֲבֹר עַמְּךָ יְהֹוָה   עַד־יַעֲבֹר עַם־זוּ
קָנִיתָ: 17   תְּבִאֵמוֹ וְתִטָּעֵמוֹ בְּהַר נַחֲלָתְךָ   מָכוֹן
לְשִׁבְתְּךָ פָּעַלְתָּ יְהֹוָה   מִקְּדָשׁ אֲדֹנָי כּוֹנְנוּ
יָדֶיךָ: 18   יְהֹוָה | יִמְלֹךְ לְעֹלָם וָעֶד:
19

43

 **At the Root**

The word בַּקֹּדֶשׁ is built on the root קדשׁ.

Words built on the root קדשׁ have **holy** as part of their meaning.

Write the three root letters in בַּקֹּדֶשׁ. ____ ____ ____

What does בַּקֹּדֶשׁ mean? _____

Read these words aloud. Then circle the three root letters in each word.

קָדוֹשׁ   נְקַדֵשׁ   הַקָדוֹשׁ   קִדְּשָׁנוּ   וַיְקַדֵשׁ

Across the Sea

Cross the Sea of Reeds in just five steps! Start at the top row and trace a shortcut by finding the Hebrew for the five English words or phrases below. Move down one line at a time.

1. who is like You   2. among the gods   3. in holiness   4. splendor   5. wonder(s)

44

 **Language Link**

The word פֶּלֶא ("wonder") not only appears in the מִי כָמֹכָה, it is also used in everyday Hebrew. Below are a few examples.

wonderful! fantastic!	נִפְלָא
wonders	נִפְלָאוֹת
cell phone	פֶּלֶאפוֹן

Help Ben tell his friend Danny about his biking experience by completing these sentences using the appropriate Hebrew words from the list above.

Ben called Danny's _____. "My front wheel brushed against Batya's back wheel," Ben said. "So I short stopped and did a hand spring off the handle bars. I landed on my feet without a scratch. It was _____, one of the most awesome _____ of my life!"

Ring, Write, and Read!

Draw a circle around one word on each line that is built on a different root than the others. Copy the circled words in the correct order on the lines below. Read aloud what you have written. Write the matching line number from the prayer on page 41. _____

1. קָדוֹשׁ   הַקָּדוֹשׁ   צוּר   קִדְּשָׁנוּ   וַיְקַדֵּשׁ

2. וְאָהַבְתָּ   אַהֲבָה   אוֹהֵב   יִשְׂרָאֵל   אַהֲבַת

3. הַמְבָרֵךְ   קוֹמָה   בָּרוּךְ   בָּרְכוּ   בְּרוּכִים

4. בְּעֶזְרַת   מֶלֶךְ   מַלְכָּה   מַלְכוּת   יִמְלֹךְ

5. זִכָּרוֹן   זֵכֶר   וְנַזְכִּיר   יִשְׂרָאֵל   וְזָכוֹר

_____   _____   _____   _____

A Legend and a Miracle

According to legend, more than two thousand years ago, the Jewish leader Judah called out the first four words of the מִי כָמֹכָה to rally the Jewish people to fight King Antiochus and regain their religious freedom. The first letter of each word became the freedom fighter's name—Maccabee.

Write the first letter of each Hebrew word in the spaces below.

מִי כָמֹכָה בָּאֵלִם יְיָ

What word does this spell? _____ _____ _____ _____

Some say it was a miracle that the small band of Maccabees defeated a great and powerful army. Which holiday celebrates their victory? _____

Do you think that the opening words of the מִי כָמֹכָה were a good rallying cry for the Jews? Why or why not?

_____

_____

Ḥanukkah Light

Read the Hebrew words below. Write the number of the matching English word above each Hebrew word.

◯   ◯   ◯   ◯

יְיָ   תְּהִלֹת   בַּקֹדֶשׁ   מִי כָמֹכָה

◯   ◯   ◯   ◯   ◯

יִשְׂרָאֵל   נִפְלָא   בָּאֵלִם   פֶּלֶא   מַכַּבִּי

1. Maccabee
2. wonderful! fantastic!
3. Israel
4. who is like you
5. among the gods
6. splendor, praises
7. wonder(s)
8. Adonai
9. in holiness

46

Bicycle Race

Play with a partner. Begin at START, reading each word out loud. When you reach a word on a yellow space, give the meaning of the word in English. If you read incorrectly or do not know the English meaning, it is your partner's turn.

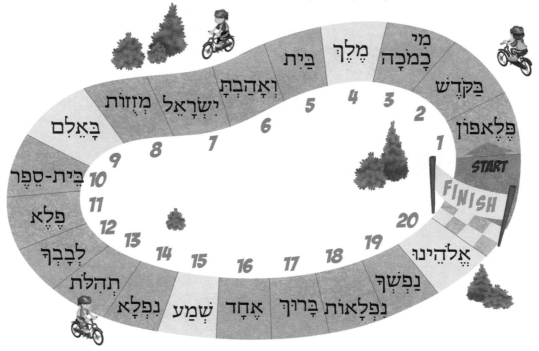

Clue to Cyberspace

One word on each line is built on a different root from the other two words. Circle that word, then copy it in the blank space below. Read the sentence you have written.

1. מִי קָדוֹשׁ קָדוֹשׁ

2. גְּאוּלִים כָּמֹכָה גְּאַלֵנוּ

3. אַהֲבָה נֶאְדָּר וְאָהַבְתָּ

4. יִמְלֹךְ מֶלֶךְ בַּקֹּדֶשׁ

1. _____ 2. _____ 3. _____ 4. _____

Which word above is the name of a prayer recited at the Shabbat table? _____

Use this clue to score bonus points in the "Tile Tip" game in Lesson 5—
מִי כָמֹכָה—on your computer.

Ben and Batya love Rabbi Lando. He thinks they're terrific, too. When he was a young rabbi their mom was one of the first students he helped prepare to become a bat mitzvah. "I enjoyed working with your mother and I look forward to working with you," Rabbi Lando said.

Name someone who remembers your mom or dad as a child. _____

Do you think that knowing your family for so long helps that person feel close to you? Explain your answer. _____

_____

Does it help you feel closer to that person? Explain your answer. _____

_____

The אָבוֹת וְאִמָּהוֹת is the first blessing of the עֲמִידָה—the central prayer in every prayer service. Jews have recited the עֲמִידָה for more than 2,000 years.

The אָבוֹת וְאִמָּהוֹת asks God to watch over us, protect us, and bless us, just as God took care of our fathers, or patriarchs (אָבוֹת)—Abraham, Isaac, and Jacob— and our mothers, or matriarchs (אִמָּהוֹת)— Sarah, Rebecca, Leah, and Rachel.

How do you feel knowing that the Jewish people's relationship with God goes back thousands of years to our ancestors in the Land of Israel?

Practice reading the אָבוֹת וְאִמָּהוֹת.

1. בָּרוּךְ אַתָּה, יְיָ, אֱלֹהֵינוּ וֵאלֹהֵי אֲבוֹתֵינוּ וְאִמּוֹתֵינוּ,

2. אֱלֹהֵי אַבְרָהָם, אֱלֹהֵי יִצְחָק, וֵאלֹהֵי יַעֲקֹב, אֱלֹהֵי שָׂרָה,

3. אֱלֹהֵי רִבְקָה, אֱלֹהֵי רָחֵל וֵאלֹהֵי לֵאָה.

4. הָאֵל הַגָּדוֹל, הַגִּבּוֹר, וְהַנּוֹרָא, אֵל עֶלְיוֹן.

5. גּוֹמֵל חֲסָדִים טוֹבִים, וְקוֹנֵה הַכֹּל,

6. וְזוֹכֵר חַסְדֵי אָבוֹת וְאִמָּהוֹת,

7. וּמֵבִיא גּוֹאֵל/גְּאֻלָּה לִבְנֵי בְנֵיהֶם,

8. לְמַעַן שְׁמוֹ, בְּאַהֲבָה. מֶלֶךְ עוֹזֵר וּמוֹשִׁיעַ וּמָגֵן.

9. בָּרוּךְ אַתָּה, יְיָ, מָגֵן אַבְרָהָם וּפֹקֵד/וְעֶזְרַת שָׂרָה.

1. *Praised are You, Adonai, our God and God of our fathers and mothers,*
2. *God of Abraham, God of Isaac, and God of Jacob, God of Sarah,*
3. *God of Rebecca, God of Rachel and God of Leah.*
4. *The great, mighty, and awesome God, supreme God.*
5. *You do acts of loving-kindness and create everything*
6. *and remember the kindnesses of the fathers and mothers,*
7. *and You will bring a redeemer/redemption to their children's children*
8. *for the sake of Your name, and in love. Ruler, Helper, Rescuer, and Shield.*
9. *Praised are You, Adonai, Shield of Abraham and Protector/Helper of Sarah.*

Prayer Variations

Some congregations pray for God to bring a redeemer (גּוֹאֵל)—the Messiah—who will bring peace to the world, while other congregations pray for redemption (גְּאֻלָּה)—a state of peace and perfection in the world. But all Jews are alike in praying for a better and more peaceful world.

Some congregations express God's loyalty to Sarah by describing God as her Protector (וְעֶזְרַת שָׂרָה). Others speak of God as Sarah's helper (וּפֹקֵד שָׂרָה). In some congregations the blessing contains only the אָבוֹת, the fathers, and not the אִמָּהוֹת, the mothers.

Prayer Words

Practice reading these words from the אָבוֹת וְאִמָּהוֹת prayer.

mothers (matriarchs, ancestors)	אִמָּהוֹת	fathers (patriarchs, ancestors)	אָבוֹת
our mothers	אִמוֹתֵינוּ	our fathers	אֲבוֹתֵינוּ
Sarah	שָׂרָה	God of	אֱלֹהֵי
Rebecca	רִבְקָה	Abraham	אַבְרָהָם
Rachel	רָחֵל	Isaac	יִצְחָק
Leah	לֵאָה	Jacob	יַעֲקֹב

✏️ Write and Read

Write the correct Hebrew word on each line below, then read the complete line.

1. בָּרוּךְ אַתָּה, יְיָ, אֱלֹהֵינוּ וֵאלֹהֵי _____ (our fathers)

   וְ _____ (our mothers)

2. אֱלֹהֵי _____ (Abraham), אֱלֹהֵי _____ (Isaac),

   וֵאלֹהֵי _____ (Jacob)

3. אֱלֹהֵי _____ (Sarah), אֱלֹהֵי _____ (Rebecca),

   אֱלֹהֵי _____ (Rachel), וֵאלֹהֵי _____ (Leah)

Unscramble the names of our ancestors.

1. חָקִיְצָ ___ ___ ___ ___

2. רָשָׂה ___ ___ ___

3. קָהרִבְ ___ ___ ___ ___

4. רָאַבְהָם ___ ___ ___ ___ ___

5. אָהֵל ___ ___ ___

Now write the first letter of each name in the blank spaces below to discover a hidden word. Do not include vowels.

___ ___ ___ ___ ___ *is the homeland of the Jewish people.*
 5   4   3   2   1

Purple or Green?

Read the words below. Write the words that describe something masculine on the purple lines. Write the words that describe something feminine on the green lines. Write the remaining word and its English meaning on the black line.

אֱלֹהֵי יִצְחָק שָׂרָה אַבְרָהָם אִמָּהוֹת אָבוֹת

רִבְקָה אִמוֹתֵנוּ אֲבוֹתֵנוּ לֵאָה רָחֵל יַעֲקֹב

___ ___ ___

___ ___

___ ___ ___

___ ___ ___

___

Judaism's First Family Tree

Unlike the American first family in Washington D.C., which changes every four or eight years, the members of Judaism's first family never change. They are always Abraham and Sarah, Isaac and Rebecca, and Jacob, Leah, and Rachel.

Fill in the missing English names on Judaism's First Family Tree.

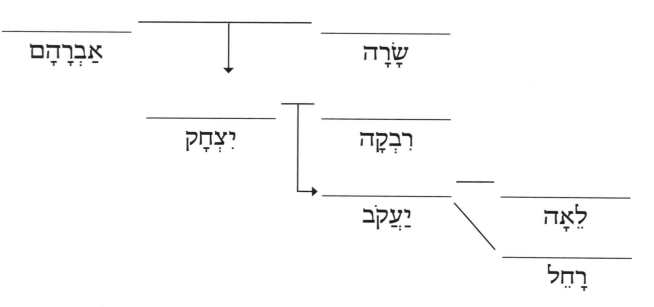

אַבְרָהָם   שָׂרָה

יִצְחָק   רִבְקָה

יַעֲקֹב   לֵאָה

רָחֵל

An important part of the אָבוֹת וְאִמָהוֹת is the belief in the merit of our ancestors (זְכוּת אָבוֹת וְאִמָהוֹת). This tradition teaches that we often receive God's protection and love because of our ancestors' goodness. What acts of goodness can *you* carry out?

יִצְחָק וְיַעֲקֹב

What's in a Name?

How many names do you have? A first name, a middle name, a last name, a Hebrew name, a nickname? Each name tells us something about you: who your family is, how your friends see you, or what your parents wished for you when you were born. The עֲמִידָה too has different names. Each tells us something more about the prayer.

- עֲמִידָה ("standing"): We stand respectfully when reciting the עֲמִידָה for we are standing before God.

- שְׁמוֹנֶה עֶשְׂרֵה ("eighteen"): Originally, the weekday version of the עֲמִידָה contained eighteen blessings. Now, the weekday עֲמִידָה includes nineteen blessings. The עֲמִידָה recited on שַׁבָּת and holidays contains seven blessings. The first three blessings and the last three blessings are almost always the same. Only the middle blessing(s) are different depending on when they are said.

- הַתְּפִלָּה ("the prayer"): The עֲמִידָה is so important that whenever the Talmud refers to "the prayer" it means the עֲמִידָה. That is why some congregations call the Amidah הַתְּפִלָּה ("the prayer").

Congregations traditionally face east—toward Jerusalem—when they recite the עֲמִידָה. Frequently, the Ark is placed to the east, so the congregants face the Ark.

The seven blessings of the עֲמִידָה on שַׁבָּת and holidays are:

1. אָבוֹת וְאִמָּהוֹת   2. גְּבוּרוֹת   3. קְדוּשָׁה   4. קְדוּשַׁת הַיּוֹם

5. עֲבוֹדָה   6. הוֹדָאָה   7. בִּרְכַּת שָׁלוֹם

Prayer Words

Practice reading these words from the אָבוֹת וְאִמָּהוֹת.

the great	הַגָּדוֹל
the mighty	הַגִּבּוֹר
and the awesome	וְהַנּוֹרָא
supreme	עֶלְיוֹן
acts of loving-kindness	חֲסָדִים טוֹבִים
helper	עוֹזֵר
and rescuer	וּמוֹשִׁיעַ
and shield	וּמָגֵן

Siddur Challenge

Write the number of each Hebrew word next to the matching English word. You will have four Hebrew words left. Unscramble them to form a siddur phrase.

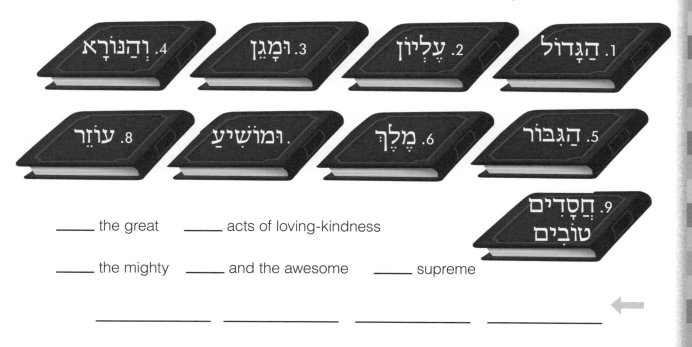

4. וְהַנּוֹרָא   3. וּמָגֵן   2. עֶלְיוֹן   1. הַגָּדוֹל

8. עוֹזֵר   . וּמוֹשִׁיעַ   6. מֶלֶךְ   5. הַגִּבּוֹר

9. חֲסָדִים טוֹבִים

_____ the great   _____ acts of loving-kindness

_____ the mighty   _____ and the awesome   _____ supreme

_____ _____ _____ _____

Super Challenge: Whom does the phrase above describe? _____

 **Pass the Pencil**

Work in a group of three. Read the first line out loud, and, if correct, check it off with a pencil, then pass the pencil to the next person. The second person reads the next line, checks it off, and so on. Change the order of readers and repeat the activity until each person in your group has read every line.

1. לְמַעַן שְׁמוֹ, בְּאַהֲבָה ☐

2. אֱלֹהֵי אַבְרָהָם, אֱלֹהֵי יִצְחָק, וֵאלֹהֵי יַעֲקֹב ☐

3. וְזוֹכֵר חַסְדֵי אָבוֹת וְאִמָּהוֹת ☐

4. גּוֹמֵל חֲסָדִים טוֹבִים, וְקוֹנֵה הַכֹּל ☐

5. מֶלֶךְ עוֹזֵר וּמוֹשִׁיעַ וּמָגֵן ☐

6. וֵאלֹהֵי אֲבוֹתֵינוּ וְאִמּוֹתֵינוּ ☐

♥ Acts of Loving-Kindness

Put a check next to the sentences below that describe חֲסָדִים טוֹבִים ("acts of loving-kindness").

1. Welcome a new student into your class.
2. Serve a hot meal at a soup kitchen.
3. Watch a movie on TV.
4. Provide the needy with warm coats in the winter.
5. Plant flowers in your garden in the spring.

Think of your own act of loving-kindness, and write it here:

_____

Putting It in ConTEXT

Before beginning the עֲמִידָה we recite these words from Psalms 51:17.

אֲדֹנָי, שְׂפָתַי תִּפְתָּח וּפִי יַגִּיד תְּהִלָּתֶךָ.

Adonai, open my lips so that my mouth may declare Your praise.

One explanation for why we recite these words is that standing before God we might feel too awed to speak. These words are a plea for support when reciting the עֲמִידָה.

Notice that unlike most prayers, Psalms 51:17 says "my lips" and "my mouth," not "our lips," and "our mouths." These words help make saying the עֲמִידָה more personal.

God's Greatness

The first row of words below describes God's **greatness**. The second describes God's **support** for us. In each row choose a word and explain why you think it is a powerful description of God.

הַגָּדוֹל	הַגִּבּוֹר	וְהַנּוֹרָא	עֶלְיוֹן .1
the great	the mighty	and the awesome	supreme

מֶלֶךְ	עוֹזֵר	וּמוֹשִׁיעַ	וּמָגֵן .2
ruler	helper	and rescuer	and shield

Line 1: _____

Why I chose this word: _____

Line 2: _____

Why I chose this word: _____

Know Before Whom You Stand

The following words are written on the Ark in many synagogues:

דַע לִפְנֵי מִי אַתָּה עוֹמֵד ("Know before whom you stand"). This reminds us to be respectful as we stand before God. When we recite the עֲמִידָה it is as if we are in the presence of a great ruler (מֶלֶךְ). In some synagogues we:

1. Stand and face east, toward Jerusalem.

2. Take three small steps backward then forward before we begin.

3. Bow several times during the עֲמִידָה.

4. Do not talk to others in the middle of reciting the עֲמִידָה.

5. Take three small steps backward when we finish the prayer.

Which actions are part of your congregation's practice? _____

_____

How might these actions influence how you feel when you pray? _____

_____

עֲמִידָה

Tic-Tac-Toe

Play Tic-Tac-Toe with a classmate. Take turns reading a word and saying its meaning. If you are correct, lightly write an X or an O in pencil in that box.

①

עֶלְיוֹן	הַמְבָרֵךְ	בַּקֹּדֶשׁ
אִמּוֹתֵינוּ	וּמוֹשִׁיעַ	יִשְׂרָאֵל
הַגָּדוֹל	יָדֶיךָ	חֲסָדִים טוֹבִים

②

הַמְּאוֹרוֹת	עוֹזֵר	אֲבוֹתֵינוּ
מֶלֶךְ	וְאָהַבְתָּ	הַגִבּוֹר
וּמָגֵן	וְהַנּוֹרָא	יִמְלֹךְ

Prayer Picture

What does the word עֲמִידָה mean? _____

Draw a picture of yourself saying this prayer. What are you doing?

_____ Which direction are you facing?

_____ Why? _____

```


```

Clue to Cyberspace

Fill in the missing letters in the prayer sentences below.

1. בָּרוּךְ אַתָּה יְיָ אֱלֹהֵ___נוּ וֵאלֹהֵי אֲ___וֹתֵינוּ וְאִמּוֹתֵינוּ

2. הָאֵל ___גָּדוֹל, הַגִבּוֹר, וְהַנּוֹרָא, אֵל עֶלְיוֹן

3. גּוֹמֵל חֲסָדִים טוֹבִי___ וְקוֹ___ה הַכֹּל

The letters you wrote form a word on line 7 of the prayer on page 49. Unscramble the letters to find the word.

Write the Hebrew word. ____ ____ ____ ____ ____

Now circle the word in the lines above that describes Abraham, Isaac, and Jacob.

Use this clue to score bonus points in the "Balloon Float" game in Lesson 6— אָבוֹת וְאִמָּהוֹת—on your computer.

"I feel g-r-r-rumpy," said Ben as he and Batya got ready for Hebrew school. "I can't believe that I missed such an easy word in the spelling bee."

"Just wait 'til Cantor Kay gets us singing and you'll be fine," said Batya, "I love when she calls out, 'One more time—but with spirit!' and we get to sing in our loudest voices. It's like jumping into a pool on a boiling hot day. I feel happy all over." ▰▰

What cheers you up and revives your spirits when you are sad or upset?

_____

Describe a time when you helped revive someone's spirits. _____

_____

Why might people pray when their spirits need to be revived? _____

_____

The גְּבוּרוֹת ("Powers") is the second blessing in the עֲמִידָה. It celebrates God's power in nature and praises God's power to give life and to free captives. It also praises God's kindness and compassion.

Why do you think it is important that when you have power you should also show kindness and compassion?

_____

_____

Practice reading the גְּבוּרוֹת.

1. אַתָּה גִבּוֹר לְעוֹלָם, אֲדֹנָי, מְחַיֵּה הַכֹּל/מֵתִים אַתָּה,
   רַב לְהוֹשִׁיעַ.

מוֹרִיד הַטָּל. —Summer   מַשִּׁיב הָרוּחַ וּמוֹרִיד הַגָּשֶׁם. —Winter

2. מְכַלְכֵּל חַיִּים בְּחֶסֶד, מְחַיֵּה הַכֹּל/מֵתִים בְּרַחֲמִים רַבִּים,

3. סוֹמֵךְ נוֹפְלִים, וְרוֹפֵא חוֹלִים, וּמַתִּיר אֲסוּרִים,

4. וּמְקַיֵּם אֱמוּנָתוֹ לִישֵׁנֵי עָפָר.

5. מִי כָמוֹךָ, בַּעַל גְּבוּרוֹת, וּמִי דוֹמֶה לָּךְ,

6. מֶלֶךְ מֵמִית וּמְחַיֶּה וּמַצְמִיחַ יְשׁוּעָה?

7. וְנֶאֱמָן אַתָּה לְהַחֲיוֹת הַכֹּל/מֵתִים.

8. בָּרוּךְ אַתָּה, יְיָ, מְחַיֵּה הַכֹּל/הַמֵּתִים.

1. *You are eternally mighty (powerful), Adonai, You give life to all/the dead,*
   great is Your power to save.
   Winter—You cause the wind to blow and the rain to fall.
   Summer—You cause the dew to fall.
2. *With kindness You sustain the living, with great compassion (mercy) give life*
   to all/the dead.
3. *You support the falling, and heal the sick, and You free the captive,*
4. *and keep faith with those who sleep in the dust.*
5. *Who is like You, Powerful One, and who is comparable to You,*
6. *Ruler who brings death and gives life and who is a source of salvation?*
7. *You are faithful to give life to all/the dead.*
8. *Blessed are You, Adonai, who gives life to all/the dead.*

Prayer Variations

Many Reform and Reconstructionist prayer books use the phrases מְחַיֵּה הַכֹּל and
מְחַיֵּה כָּל חַי ("gives life to everything"). Conservative and Orthodox prayer books
use מְחַיֵּה מֵתִים ("revives the dead"). *Mishkan T'filah,* the Reform prayer book,
gives the option of מְחַיֵּה מֵתִים or מְחַיֵּה הַכֹּל.

Some prayer books add one line in the winter and a different line in the summer.

Prayer Words

Practice reading these words from the גְּבוּרוֹת.

mighty, powerful	גִּבּוֹר
life	חַיִּים
with kindness	בְּחֶסֶד
with compassion, mercy	בְּרַחֲמִים
gives life	מְחַיֶּה
Powerful One	בַּעַל גְּבוּרוֹת

🔍 Clue Copy

Write the Hebrew word for each English meaning.

Powerful One   ___ ___ ___ ___ ___   ___ ___ ◯ .1

mighty, powerful   ___ ◯ ___ ___ ___ .2

with kindness   ___ ___ ◯ .3

with compassion, mercy   ___ ___ ◯ ___ ___ .4

gives life   ___ ◯ ___ .5

life   ◯ ___ ___ ___ .6

Now copy the letters from the circles to the lines below to complete the prayer phrase.

רַבִּים ___ ___ ___ ___ ___ ___

Lively Words

מְחַיֶּה means **gives life**.

The root of מְחַיֶּה is חיה.

The root letters חיה tell us that **life** is part of a word's meaning. When ה is the final root letter it is sometimes missing in a word.

Circle the words below that have the root חיה.

חַיֵּינוּ   רַחֲמִים   חַי   חַיּוֹת   חַיָּה   וִיחֻנֶּךָ   חַיִּים

The Hebrew lines below are so full of life, you may want to sing them. Practice reading—then sing if you like.

1. עַם יִשְׂרָאֵל חַי. עוֹד אָבִינוּ חַי.

2. דָּוִד מֶלֶךְ יִשְׂרָאֵל חַי וְקַיָּם.

One interpretation of מְחַיֶּה הַמֵּתִים is the belief that everyone who has died will be brought back to life by God in the future. A different interpretation is that spring's awakening of dormant plants and hibernating animals is God's way of bringing Creation back to life. But whatever their interpretation is of מְחַיֶּה הַמֵּתִים, most Jews believe that God gave each of us a soul (נֶפֶשׁ) that lives forever.

Finding our Place

Here are the seven בְּרָכוֹת of the עֲמִידָה for Shabbat and holidays. Circle the name of the בְּרָכָה that means "powers."

1. אָבוֹת וְאִמָּהוֹת   2. גְּבוּרוֹת   3. קְדוּשָׁה   4. קְדוּשַׁת הַיּוֹם

5. עֲבוֹדָה   6. הוֹדָאָה   7. בִּרְכַּת שָׁלוֹם

Which בְּרָכָה names the patriarchs and matriarchs? Write your answer in עִבְרִית (Hebrew) and English.

English: _____   _____ :עִבְרִית

Search and Circle

Circle the English meaning of each Hebrew word.

Abraham	our mothers	our fathers	1. אִמּוֹתֵינוּ
holiness	ancestors	the mighty	2. הַגִּבּוֹר
and shield	gives life	the great	3. מְחַיֶּה
blessed	life	ruler	4. חַיִּים
Powerful One	helper	with kindness	5. בַּעַל גְּבוּרוֹת

 Pass the Pencil

Work in a group of three. Read the first line out loud, and, if correct, check it off with a pencil, then pass the pencil to the next person. The second person reads the next line, checks it off, and so on. Change the order of readers and repeat the activity until each person in your group has read every line.

1. ☐ מְכַלְכֵּל חַיִּים בְּחֶסֶד, מְחַיֶּה הַכֹּל/מֵתִים בְּרַחֲמִים רַבִּים

2. ☐ מִי כָמוֹךָ, בַּעַל גְּבוּרוֹת, וּמִי דוֹמֶה לָּךְ

3. ☐ מֶלֶךְ מֵמִית וּמְחַיֶּה וּמַצְמִיחַ יְשׁוּעָה

4. ☐ מַשִּׁיב הָרוּחַ וּמוֹרִיד הַגָּשֶׁם

5. ☐ סוֹמֵךְ נוֹפְלִים, וְרוֹפֵא חוֹלִים, וּמַתִּיר אֲסוּרִים

 **Language Link**

Here is some health-wise Hebrew. Each word or phrase below is built on the root רפא.
Words built on the root letters רפא have **healing** as part of their meaning.

Practice reading these words.

doctor (masc, fem)	רוֹפֵא, רוֹפְאָה
infirmary, clinic	מִרְפָּאָה
[Wishing you a] full recovery!	רְפוּאָה שְׁלֵמָה

Find the phrase in the גְּבוּרוֹת on page 61 that means "and heal the sick" and write it
here. _____

 Jewish tradition teaches that God heals the sick and that people can
follow in God's ways. The mitzvah of visiting the sick (בִּקוּר חוֹלִים)
lets us comfort those who are ill, for example, by offering a kind word, a
funny book, or a handmade gift. How can you cheer up a friend who is ill?

Who or What Am I?

Fill in the blanks using the appropriate Hebrew words from "Language Link" above.

1. I'm where summer campers go when they break an arm or toe. _____

2. I'm your pal when you're in pain. I can heal any sprain. _____

3. I'm the wish that you be well when you got hurt because you fell. _____

רְפוּאָה שְׁלֵמָה

Putting It in ConTEXT

There is a special prayer asking for healing. Traditionally it is recited during the Torah service on שַׁבָּת. But you can recite it whenever you want to pray for someone who is ill. It is called the מִי שֶׁבֵּרַךְ.

Practice reading this version of the מִי שֶׁבֵּרַךְ.

1. מִי שֶׁבֵּרַךְ אֲבוֹתֵינוּ וְאִמּוֹתֵינוּ, אַבְרָהָם יִצְחָק וְיַעֲקֹב, שָׂרָה רִבְקָה רָחֵל וְלֵאָה,

2. הוּא יְבָרֵךְ וִירַפֵּא אֶת הַחוֹלֶה _____ בֶּן _____ / הַחוֹלָה _____ בַּת _____.

3. הַקָּדוֹשׁ בָּרוּךְ הוּא יִמָּלֵא רַחֲמִים עָלָיו, לְהַחֲזִיקוֹ וּלְרַפְּאוֹתוֹ /עָלֶיהָ, לְהַחֲזִיקָהּ וּלְרַפְּאוֹתָהּ,

4. וְיִשְׁלַח לוֹ/לָהּ מְהֵרָה רְפוּאָה שְׁלֵמָה מִן הַשָּׁמַיִם,

5. רְפוּאַת הַנֶּפֶשׁ, וּרְפוּאַת הַגּוּף,

6. בְּתוֹךְ שְׁאָר חוֹלֵי יִשְׂרָאֵל, וְנֹאמַר אָמֵן.

1. *May God who blessed our ancestors, Abraham, Isaac, and Jacob, Sarah, Rebecca, Rachel and Leah,*
2. *bless and heal _____ son of _____ / daughter of _____ who is ill.*
3. *May the Holy Blessed One be compassionate and strengthen and heal him/her,*
4. *and speedily send him/her a complete recovery,*
5. *both spiritual and physical,*
6. *together with all others who are ill. And let us say, Amen.*

Underline the Hebrew names of the patriarchs and matriarchs in the מִי שֶׁבֵּרַךְ.

Circle each Hebrew word that is built on the root רפא. How many words did you find? _____

Why do you think there are so many words built on this root in the מִי שֶׁבֵּרַךְ?

_____

 **At the Root**

בְּרַחֲמִים means **with compassion** or **with mercy.**

Explain in your own words what "compassion" and "mercy" mean.

_____

בְּ means _____

רַחֲמִים means _____

The root of בְּרַחֲמִים is רחמ.

The root רחמ tells us that **compassion** or **mercy** is part of a word's meaning.

God is sometimes called אֵל מָלֵא רַחֲמִים. Fill in the missing English translation:

God full of _____

Here are three other names by which God is known. Circle the root רחמ in each phrase.

אַב הָרַחֲמִים   אֵל רַחוּם וְחַנּוּן   הָרַחֲמָן

Merciful Parent   Compassionate and Gracious God   The Merciful One

Which of the four names above do you like best to describe God? Why?

_____

The Talmud tells us that if we expect compassion from God, we need to show compassion to others. Give an example of how you might show compassion to someone else.

_____

_____

WANTED: HEROES

In the גְבוּרוֹת we say to God: אַתָּה גִבּוֹר, "You are powerful." גִבּוֹר means both "powerful" and "hero." Jewish tradition teaches that although no one can be God, everyone can be one of God's heroes. For example, God provides the world with sunshine and rain, and people can take care of the earth and its creatures by helping to feed the hungry or teaching people how to irrigate their land.

If God wrote a job ad for a hero what might it say? _____

_____

_____

Would your job ad be different? How?

_____

_____

What do you think the best part of the job would be? The worst?

Best: _____

Worst: _____

Describe one step you can take to be a hero to someone else. _____

_____

God is sometimes called הַגְבוּרָה. What do you think that means? Why do you think we give God that name?

 **Growing Roots**

Write each word above its root in the drawings below.

הָרַחֲמָן רְפוּאָה קָדְשׁוֹ חַיִּים

נִפְלָא קִדְּשָׁנוּ מְחַיֶּה רַחוּם חַיּוֹת

רוֹפֵא וַיְקַדֵּשׁ הַקָּדוֹשׁ מִרְפָּאָה

——————

———— ———— ————

———— ———— ————

———— ————

פלא   רחם   קדש   רפא   חיה

לְחַיִּים!

Abracadabra!

"Abracadabra" is a shortened version of *avara k'davara*, a phrase in Aramaic—the ancient language that is similar to Hebrew and in which much of the Talmud is written. It means "I create as I speak." A midrash says that this reminds us of the Jewish belief that God's power (גְּבוּרָה) is in the letters and words of prayer.

 Reading Race

Play with a partner. Begin at START, reading each word out loud. When you reach a word on a yellow space, give the meaning of the word in English. If you read incorrectly or do not know the English meaning, it is your partner's turn.

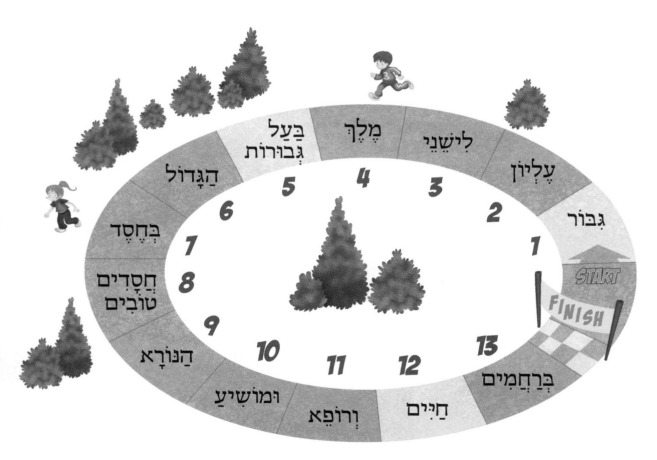

Clue to Cyberspace

וּמְחַיֶּה   חַיִּים   מְחַיֶּה   לְהַחֲיוֹת

Write the root on which these words are built. _____ _____ _____

Write the general meaning of these words. _____

Now choose the correct word from the list above to complete each sentence below. Each time you use a word, put a check next to the leaf. **Hint 1:** You will use one of the words three times. Put checks next to that leaf each additional time you use the word. **Hint 2:** If you need help, turn to page 61.

1. אַתָּה גִבּוֹר לְעוֹלָם, אֲדֹנָי, _____ הַכֹּל/מֵתִים
   אַתָּה, רַב לְהוֹשִׁיעַ.

2. מְכַלְכֵּל _____ בְּחֶסֶד, _____ הַכֹּל/מֵתִים
   בְּרַחֲמִים רַבִּים.

3. מִי כָמוֹךָ, בַּעַל גְּבוּרוֹת, וּמִי דוֹמֶה לָּךְ, מֶלֶךְ מֵמִית
   _____.

4. וְנֶאֱמָן אַתָּה _____ הַכֹּל/מֵתִים.

5. בָּרוּךְ אַתָּה, יְיָ, _____ הַכֹּל/הַמֵּתִים.

Which Hebrew word in the leaves means "life"? _____

Use this clue to score bonus points in the "Carnival Duck!" game in
Lesson 7—גְּבוּרוֹת—on your computer.

Ben gave Batya a great birthday present—a metallic red pen that shimmered in the sunlight. Best of all, he had Batya's name engraved in gold letters along its side. She was thrilled.

The pen was like no other—the only one of its kind—and Batya treated it that way. She kept it in its own case, separate from her other pens and pencils.

Name something that you value so much that you keep it separate. Perhaps you set it aside for use only on certain occasions or care for it in a special way.

_____

Why do you value this item? How do you treat it?

_____

_____

The קְדוּשָׁה ("Holiness") prayer is the third בְּרָכָה in the Shabbat morning עֲמִידָה. The theme of the קְדוּשָׁה is God's holiness, which makes God separate and different from everything else. When we recite this prayer, we declare that God is holy and we praise God's glory and greatness.

How does going to synagogue to pray as a community honor God?

_____

Putting It in ConTEXT

At the heart of the קְדוּשָׁה are three verses that come from different parts of the תָּנָ"ךְ (the Bible). Practice reading those verses in preparation for learning the קְדוּשָׁה.

1. קָדוֹשׁ, קָדוֹשׁ, קָדוֹשׁ יְיָ צְבָאוֹת, מְלֹא כָל-הָאָרֶץ כְּבוֹדוֹ.
(Isaiah 6:3)

2. בָּרוּךְ כְּבוֹד יְיָ מִמְּקוֹמוֹ. (Ezekiel 3:12)

3. יִמְלֹךְ יְיָ לְעוֹלָם, אֱלֹהַיִךְ צִיּוֹן, לְדֹר וָדֹר, הַלְלוּיָהּ!
(Psalms 146:10)

In the first verse, the prophet Isaiah describes a beautiful vision of God sitting on the divine throne, surrounded by angels. As the angels move their wings, they call to one another:

קָדוֹשׁ, קָדוֹשׁ, קָדוֹשׁ יְיָ צְבָאוֹת, מְלֹא כָל-הָאָרֶץ כְּבוֹדוֹ.

Holy, Holy, Holy is Adonai of the heavenly legions, the whole earth is full of God's glory.

Why might reciting the words of the angels help us feel closer to God?

_____

How might it help us feel closer to the other members of our synagogue community?

_____

Describe something else we can do to help us feel closer to i) God and ii) our community.

i) God: _____

ii) Community: _____

Practice reading the קְדוּשָׁה.

1. נְקַדֵּשׁ אֶת שִׁמְךָ בָּעוֹלָם, כְּשֵׁם שֶׁמַּקְדִּישִׁים אוֹתוֹ בִּשְׁמֵי מָרוֹם,

2. כַּכָּתוּב עַל יַד נְבִיאֶךָ: וְקָרָא זֶה אֶל זֶה וְאָמַר:

3. קָדוֹשׁ, קָדוֹשׁ, קָדוֹשׁ יְיָ צְבָאוֹת, מְלֹא כָל־הָאָרֶץ כְּבוֹדוֹ.

4. אַדִּיר אַדִּירֵנוּ, יְיָ אֲדוֹנֵנוּ, מָה אַדִּיר שִׁמְךָ בְּכָל הָאָרֶץ.

5. בָּרוּךְ כְּבוֹד יְיָ מִמְּקוֹמוֹ.

6. אֶחָד הוּא אֱלֹהֵינוּ, הוּא אָבִינוּ, הוּא מַלְכֵּנוּ, הוּא מוֹשִׁיעֵנוּ,

7. וְהוּא יַשְׁמִיעֵנוּ בְּרַחֲמָיו לְעֵינֵי כָּל חָי. אֲנִי יְיָ אֱלֹהֵיכֶם.

8. יִמְלֹךְ יְיָ לְעוֹלָם, אֱלֹהַיִךְ צִיּוֹן, לְדֹר וָדֹר, הַלְלוּיָהּ!

9. לְדוֹר וָדוֹר נַגִּיד גָּדְלֶךָ, וּלְנֵצַח נְצָחִים קְדֻשָּׁתְךָ נַקְדִּישׁ.

10. וְשִׁבְחֲךָ, אֱלֹהֵינוּ, מִפִּינוּ לֹא יָמוּשׁ לְעוֹלָם וָעֶד.

11. בָּרוּךְ אַתָּה, יְיָ, הָאֵל הַקָּדוֹשׁ.

1. Let us sanctify Your name in the world, as they sanctify it in the highest heavens,

2. as it is written by Your prophet, and one called to another and said:

3. "Holy, Holy, Holy is Adonai of the heavenly legions, the whole earth is full of God's glory."

4. You are majestic, Adonai, our God. How powerful is Your name throughout the earth.

5. Praised is the glory of God from God's heavenly place.

6. Our God is one, God is our parent, God is our ruler, God is our rescuer,

7. And with mercy God will declare before all the living, I am Adonai, your God.

8. Adonai will rule forever; your God, O Zion, from generation to generation. Halleluyah!

9. From generation to generation we will tell of Your greatness, and for all eternity we will proclaim Your holiness.

10. And our praise of You, O God, will not depart from our mouths forever and ever.

11. Praised are You, Adonai, the holy God.

Prayer Words

Practice reading these words from the קְדוּשָׁה prayer.

let us sanctify, make holy	נְקַדֵּשׁ
Your name	שִׁמְךָ
as it is written	כַּכָּתוּב
Your prophet	נְבִיאֶךָ
God's glory	כְּבוֹדוֹ
Zion, Israel	צִיּוֹן
from generation to generation	לְדוֹר וָדוֹר
Your greatness	גָּדְלֶךָ

 **Call Out!**

Write the Hebrew word or phrase below the matching English below.

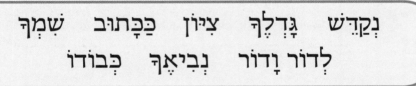

נְקַדֵּשׁ גָּדְלֶךָ צִיּוֹן כַּכָּתוּב שִׁמְךָ
לְדוֹר וָדוֹר נְבִיאֶךָ כְּבוֹדוֹ

let us sanctify, make holy	Your greatness	as it is written
_____	_____	_____

God's glory	Zion, Israel	Your prophet
_____	_____	_____

from generation to generation	Your name
_____	_____

Prayer Variations

The Reform prayer book, *Mishkan T'filah,* includes the lines beginning
אֶחָד הוּא אֱלֹהֵינוּ and אַדִּיר אַדִּירֵנוּ in the Shabbat morning service.

Finding Your Focus

The seven בְּרָכוֹת of the עֲמִידָה on Shabbat and holidays are listed below. Circle the
name of the בְּרָכָה that means "holiness."

1. אָבוֹת וְאִמָּהוֹת   2. גְּבוּרוֹת   3. קְדוּשָׁה   4. קְדוּשַׁת הַיּוֹם

5. עֲבוֹדָה   6. הוֹדָאָה   7. בִּרְכַּת שָׁלוֹם

Because the קְדוּשָׁה says that God is holy, we try to think hard about the words when
we recite it, in the same way we do when we say the שְׁמַע.

One tradition is to rise up on our toes three times as we
say קָדוֹשׁ, קָדוֹשׁ, קָדוֹשׁ, imagining that we are elevating
ourselves in the same way that the angels are elevated in
God's eyes. It is as if we are reaching toward heaven.

Praying Like an Angel

Jewish tradition teaches us that when we recite the קְדוּשָׁה we echo the angels who
sing of God's holiness and glory. So we try to approach God with the great respect that
angels show. For example, we recite the קְדוּשָׁה only when at least ten Jewish adults—a
מִנְיָן—are present. And we don't leave the sanctuary during the קְדוּשָׁה.

Give two examples of how you show respect to someone or something important.

1. _____

2. _____

 **At the Root**

קְדוּשָׁה means **holy** or **holiness**.

The root of קְדוּשָׁה is קדש.

The root קדש tells us that **holiness** is part of a word's meaning.

Circle the root letters קדש in each Hebrew word below.

נְקַדֵּשׁ   קָדוֹשׁ   נַקְדִּישׁ   הַקָּדוֹשׁ   קַדִּישׁ   קְדֻשָּׁתְךָ

Draw a wine cup around the name of the blessing over wine.

Turn to the קְדוּשָׁה on page 74 and underline each word that is built on the root letters קדש. How many words did you find? _____

Siddur Challenge

Fill in the missing קדש words from the קְדוּשָׁה to complete the phrases below. Then read the prayer out loud.

1. _____ אֶת שִׁמְךָ בָּעוֹלָם, כְּשֵׁם _____ אוֹתוֹ
בִּשְׁמֵי מָרוֹם,

2. כַּכָּתוּב עַל יַד נְבִיאֶךָ וְקָרָא זֶה אֶל זֶה וְאָמַר:

3. _____ , _____ , _____ , יְיָ צְבָאוֹת, מְלֹא
כָל־הָאָרֶץ כְּבוֹדוֹ.

Bonus: Circle the word that means "your name."

 **Language Link**

What do you think it means to have "a good name"?

_____

Jewish tradition teaches the importance of a good name, שֵׁם טוֹב, of being known as an honest, kind, and hardworking person—a mensch! Read the following quote from Rabbi Simeon in Pirkei Avot then answer the questions.

שְׁלֹשָׁה כְתָרִים הֵם: כֶּתֶר תּוֹרָה וְכֶתֶר כְּהֻנָּה וְכֶתֶר מַלְכוּת,
וְכֶתֶר שֵׁם טוֹב עוֹלֶה עַל גַּבֵּיהֶן.

There are three crowns: The crown of Torah, the crown of the priesthood, and the crown of royalty. But the crown of a good name is the greatest of all.
(Pirkei Avot 4:13).

Do you think the image of a crown is appropriate for a good name? Why or why not? What other image might you use?

_____

_____

 Our tradition also teaches that people are called by three names: the name their parents give them, the name other people give them, and the name they earn through their actions. Describe something you have done that helped you earn a שֵׁם טוֹב.

Practice reading the lines below. Then circle the word שֵׁם or a variation in each line.

1. יִהְיֶה יְיָ אֶחָד וּשְׁמוֹ אֶחָד

2. לְאַהֲבָה וּלְיִרְאָה אֶת שְׁמֶךָ

3. לְמַעַן שְׁמוֹ בְּאַהֲבָה

4. אַתָּה קָדוֹשׁ וְשִׁמְךָ קָדוֹשׁ

What's Your Name?

When you first meet people—before you get to know much about them—you usually ask what their name is. Now you can do it in Hebrew!

my name [is]	שְׁמִי
what [is]	מַה
your name (masc, fem)	שִׁמְךָ, שְׁמֵךְ
his name, her name	שְׁמוֹ, שְׁמָה

To ask a girl what her name is, say: ?מַה שְׁמֵךְ

To ask a boy say: _____

When someone asks you: ?מַה שְׁמֵךְ or ?מַה שִׁמְךָ, answer:

שְׁמִי _____.

write your name here

Turn to a classmate and in Hebrew ask his or her name. Then switch. Tell one another your names using the following phrase: שְׁמִי _____.

From Generation to Generation

Hebrew names are often passed לְדוֹר וָדוֹר ("from generation to generation").

Were you named for someone from a previous generation in your family?
If so, who? _____

Circle the Hebrew phrase meaning "from generation to generation" each time it appears in the קְדוּשָׁה on page 74.

How many phrases did you circle? _____

 **At the Root**

יִמְלֹךְ means **will rule**.

The root of יִמְלֹךְ is מלכ.

Earlier you learned that the root letters מלכ tell us that **rule** is part of a word's meaning.

Circle the words below that have the root letters מלכ. *(Remember that at the end of a word the letter כ looks like this: ךְ.)*

מֶלַח   מַלְכָּה   יִמְלֹךְ   מֶלֶךְ   מָלֵא   מַלְכוּת

Draw a crown around the word that means "ruler" or "king."

Bonus: Underline the word that means "queen." (**Hint:** The phrase שַׁבָּת הַמַּלְכָּה means "the Sabbath Queen.")

Practice reading these sentences. Then underline each word that is built on the root מלכ.

1. מֶלֶךְ עוֹזֵר וּמוֹשִׁיעַ וּמָגֵן.

2. אֵל חַי וְקַיָּם, תָּמִיד יִמְלֹךְ עָלֵינוּ לְעוֹלָם וָעֶד.

3. בָּרוּךְ אַתָּה, יְיָ אֱלֹהֵינוּ, מֶלֶךְ הָעוֹלָם, בּוֹרֵא פְּרִי הַגָּפֶן.

4. וַיָּבֹא הַמֶּלֶךְ וְהָמָן לִשְׁתּוֹת עִם-אֶסְתֵּר הַמַּלְכָּה.

5. מִמֶּלֶךְ מַלְכֵי הַמְּלָכִים, הַקָּדוֹשׁ בָּרוּךְ הוּא.

How many words did you underline? _____

Which sentence do you think is from the scroll we read on Purim? What was your clue?

_____

The symbol on the flag of Israel is called a מָגֵן דָּוִד, meaning "shield of David." It is also called a Jewish star. Which sentence above includes the Hebrew word for shield? _____

Turn to page 74 and circle the two words in the קְדוּשָׁה that are built on the root letters מלכ.

Clue to Cyberspace

Start at the bottom to climb up the wall. Complete each phrase. Draw a line from the words with the root קדש to the correct empty bricks. Choose from these words:

הַקָּדוֹשׁ   קָדוֹשׁ   קִדַּשְׁתָּ   נְקַדֵּשׁ   נַקְדִּישׁ   שֶׁמַּקְדִּישִׁים

4. בָּרוּךְ אַתָּה יְיָ הָאֵל ▯ ▯ ▯ ▯ ▯

3. לְדוֹר וָדוֹר נַגִּיד גָּדְלֶךָ וּלְנֵצַח נְצָחִים ▯ ▯ ▯ ▯

2. ▯ ▯ ▯ יְיָ צְבָאוֹת מְלֹא כָל הָאָרֶץ כְּבוֹדוֹ

1. אֶת שִׁמְךָ בָּעוֹלָם כְּשֵׁם ▯ ▯ אוֹתוֹ בִּשְׁמֵי מָרוֹם

Read all of the sentences out loud.

Which word in the lines above is the last word we say when reciting the HaMotzi blessing?_____

Use this clue to score bonus points in the "Tile Tip" game in Lesson 8— קְדוּשָׁה—on your computer.

"I'm not speaking to you," Ben announced to Batya as they arrived at synagogue. They had been arguing since they left home. Ben was upset because Batya had used his bike without permission. Now the seat tilted back in a funny way.

"Fine. Then I'll tell mom what happened on Tuesday," Batya threatened.

If you could speak with Ben and Batya, how would you help them make peace?

_____

_____

Think of a time when you were upset with someone. What helped you make peace?

_____

Jewish tradition teaches that nothing is more important than שָׁלוֹם. That is why we greet each other—and say goodbye—with the wish of שָׁלוֹם. Think about it: Can you have a strong sports team without peace among the players? How about a good friendship? A classroom where you can learn?

Why is peace so important? _____

_____

The prayers in this chapter—שָׁלוֹם רָב, שִׂים שָׁלוֹם, עֹשֶׂה שָׁלוֹם—are prayers for peace. How can you tell? They ask God to grant peace to our people and to the whole world.

The final blessing of the עֲמִידָה is a prayer for peace—בִּרְכַּת שָׁלוֹם. In the evening service, it begins with the words שָׁלוֹם רָב ("great peace"). The prayer asks God for peace in the world forever. In the morning, בִּרְכַּת שָׁלוֹם begins with a passage whose opening words are שִׂים שָׁלוֹם ("grant peace"). You will study שִׂים שָׁלוֹם later in this chapter.

שָׁלוֹם רָב

Practice reading שָׁלוֹם רָב.

1. שָׁלוֹם רָב עַל יִשְׂרָאֵל עַמְּךָ (וְעַל כָּל-יוֹשְׁבֵי תֵבֵל) תָּשִׂים לְעוֹלָם,

2. כִּי אַתָּה הוּא מֶלֶךְ אָדוֹן לְכָל הַשָּׁלוֹם.

3. וְטוֹב בְּעֵינֶיךָ לְבָרֵךְ אֶת-עַמְּךָ יִשְׂרָאֵל

4. בְּכָל-עֵת וּבְכָל-שָׁעָה בִּשְׁלוֹמֶךָ.

5. בָּרוּךְ אַתָּה, יְיָ, הַמְבָרֵךְ אֶת-עַמּוֹ יִשְׂרָאֵל בַּשָּׁלוֹם.

1. *May You grant great peace upon Israel Your people (and upon all who live on the earth) forever,*
2. *for You are the Ruler, Sovereign of all peace.*
3. *And may it be good in Your eyes to bless Your people Israel*
4. *at every time and every hour with Your peace.*
5. *Praised are You, Adonai, who blesses Your people Israel with peace.*

Prayer Variations

Some congregations include the phrase וְעַל כָּל-יוֹשְׁבֵי תֵבֵל ("and upon all who live on the earth") in the blessing for peace. Whether or not that phrase is included, we know that the prayer asks for peace for all the people of the world.

Prayer Words

Practice reading these words from שָׁלוֹם רָב.

great	רָב
Your people	עַמְּךָ
in Your eyes	בְּעֵינֶיךָ
to bless	לְבָרֵךְ
with Your peace	בִּשְׁלוֹמֶךָ
who blesses	הַמְבָרֵךְ

Search and Circle

Write the Hebrew word for each English meaning. Find the Hebrew words hidden in the word search grid. Look from right to left and top to bottom. Write the remaining letters from right to left on the blank lines to find a hidden message.

1. Israel _____

2. Your people _____

3. great _____

4. with Your peace _____

5. who blesses _____

6. in Your eyes _____

7. to bless _____

ב	ל	א	ר	שׁ	י	ב
שׁ	ל	ב	ר	ךְ	מ	ע
ל	ב	ע	ל	כ	ב	י
ו	ר	כ	ב	ו	ת	נ
מ	ךְ	ה	ע	שׁ	ל	י
ךְ	ר	ךְ	ר	ב	מ	ה

___ ___ ___ ___ ___ ___ ___ ___ ___
  ָ   ָ   ָ   :   ֵ   ָ   :

 **At the Root**

שָׁלוֹם means **peace.**

שָׁלוֹם is built on the root letters שׁלמ.

Words built on the root שׁלמ have **peace, harmony, completeness,** or **wholeness** as part of their meaning.

On Friday night at the dinner table, after we light שַׁבָּת candles, we greet the angels of peace by singing שָׁלוֹם עֲלֵיכֶם. This is the second line of the song:

בּוֹאֲכֶם לְשָׁלוֹם, מַלְאֲכֵי הַשָּׁלוֹם, מַלְאֲכֵי עֶלְיוֹן, מִמֶּלֶךְ מַלְכֵי הַמְּלָכִים, הַקָּדוֹשׁ בָּרוּךְ הוּא.

May you come in peace, angels of peace, angels from the One on high, the Ruler of rulers, the Holy Blessed One.

Circle the words that are built on the root שׁלמ in the line from שָׁלוֹם עֲלֵיכֶם. How many words did you circle? _____

The last verse of שָׁלוֹם עֲלֵיכֶם begins with the phrase צֵאתְכֶם לְשָׁלוֹם ("Depart in peace").

What might you want to say to the angels of peace on Friday night? _____

_____

צֵאתְכֶם לְשָׁלוֹם

Practice reading שִׂים שָׁלוֹם—the version of בִּרְכַּת שָׁלוֹם that we recite during the morning service.

1. שִׂים שָׁלוֹם (בָּעוֹלָם), טוֹבָה וּבְרָכָה, חֵן וָחֶסֶד וְרַחֲמִים

2. עָלֵינוּ וְעַל־כָּל־יִשְׂרָאֵל עַמֶּךָ.

3. בָּרְכֵנוּ, אָבִינוּ/יוֹצְרֵנוּ, כֻּלָּנוּ כְּאֶחָד, בְּאוֹר פָּנֶיךָ,

4. כִּי בְאוֹר פָּנֶיךָ נָתַתָּ לָּנוּ, יְיָ, אֱלֹהֵינוּ,

5. תּוֹרַת חַיִּים, וְאַהֲבַת חֶסֶד, וּצְדָקָה וּבְרָכָה

6. וְרַחֲמִים, וְחַיִּים וְשָׁלוֹם.

7. וְטוֹב בְּעֵינֶיךָ לְבָרֵךְ אֶת־עַמְּךָ יִשְׂרָאֵל

8. בְּכָל־עֵת וּבְכָל־שָׁעָה בִּשְׁלוֹמֶךָ.

9. בָּרוּךְ אַתָּה, יְיָ, הַמְבָרֵךְ אֶת־עַמּוֹ יִשְׂרָאֵל בַּשָּׁלוֹם.

1. *Grant peace (in the world), goodness and blessing, graciousness and kindness and mercy (compassion)*

2. *upon us and upon all Israel Your people.*

3. *Bless us, our Parent/Creator, all of us as one, with the light of Your face,*

4. *for with the light of Your face, Adonai our God, You gave us*

5. *the Torah of life, and a love of kindness, and righteousness and blessing*

6. *and mercy (compassion), and life and peace.*

7. *And may it be good in Your eyes to bless Your people Israel*

8. *at every time and at every hour with Your peace.*

9. *Praised are You, Adonai, who blesses Your people Israel with peace.*

Prayer Variations

Some congregations include the word בָּעוֹלָם ("in the world") to remind us that the blessing for peace is for all the people of the world. Some congregations call God אָבִינוּ "our Father" or "our Parent," while others call God יוֹצְרֵנוּ ("our Creator"). Both names express our respect for God.

Prayer Words

Practice reading these words from the שִׂים שָׁלוֹם prayer.

grant, put	שִׂים
kindness	חֶסֶד
and mercy	וְרַחֲמִים
all of us as one	כֻּלָנוּ כְּאֶחָד
Your face	פָּנֶיךָ
the Torah of life	תּוֹרַת חַיִּים
and a love of kindness	וְאַהֲבַת חֶסֶד

 Reading Riddle

Fill in the missing words, then read the prayer aloud.

1. _____ שָׁלוֹם (בָּעוֹלָם), טוֹבָה וּבְרָכָה
   grant, put

2. חֵן וָ _____ _____ עָלֵינוּ
   and mercy   kindness

   וְעַל־כָּל־יִשְׂרָאֵל עַמֶּךָ.

3. בָּרְכֵנוּ, אָבִינוּ/יוֹצְרֵנוּ, _____
                                    all of us as one

   בְּאוֹר פָּנֶיךָ

4. כִּי בְאוֹר _____ נָתַתָּ לָנוּ, יְיָ אֱלֹהֵינוּ, תּוֹרַת
              your face

   _____ וְאַהֲבַת _____,
   life   kindness

6. וּצְדָקָה וּבְרָכָה וְרַחֲמִים, וְחַיִּים וְ _____.
                                                peace

At the Root

1. The word שִׂים usually means **put**. (In שִׂים שָׁלוֹם we translate it as **grant**.)

   שִׂים is built on the root letters שׂים.

   Words built on the root שׂים have **put** as part of their meaning.

   Draw a circle around the words that are built on the root שׂים.

   שֶׁמֶן   שִׂים   שִׂמְךָ   שִׂימָה   שִׁיר   תָּשִׂים

2. The word נָתַתָּ means **you gave**.

   נָתַתָּ is built on the root letters נתן.

   Words built on the root נתן have **give** as part of their meaning.

   What root letter is missing in the word נָתַתָּ? _____

Root Roundup

Read each line below. Find and circle the words with the roots listed in the first row of the chart. Some roots appear more than once. Check the chart to make sure you have found them all!

root	שׂים	קדשׁ	שׁלמ	נתנ	מלכ
meaning	put	holy, set apart	wholeness	give	ruler, king
# times root appears	2	3	4	1	3

1. שִׂים שָׁלוֹם (בָּעוֹלָם), טוֹבָה וּבְרָכָה, חֵן וָחֶסֶד וְרַחֲמִים

2. שָׁלוֹם רָב עַל יִשְׂרָאֵל עַמְּךָ (וְעַל כָּל-יוֹשְׁבֵי תֵבֵל) תָּשִׂים לְעוֹלָם

3. נְקַדֵּשׁ אֶת שִׁמְךָ בָּעוֹלָם, כְּשֵׁם שֶׁמַּקְדִּישִׁים אוֹתוֹ בִּשְׁמֵי מָרוֹם

4. בּוֹאֲכֶם לְשָׁלוֹם, מַלְאֲכֵי הַשָּׁלוֹם, מַלְאֲכֵי עֶלְיוֹן, מִמֶּלֶךְ מַלְכֵי הַמְּלָכִים, הַקָּדוֹשׁ בָּרוּךְ הוּא

5. כִּי בְאוֹר פָּנֶיךָ נָתַתָּ לָּנוּ, יְיָ אֱלֹהֵינוּ

88

Putting It in ConTEXT

Read these words from Psalm 34:15 in Hebrew and English.

סוּר מֵרָע וַעֲשֵׂה־טוֹב בַּקֵּשׁ שָׁלוֹם וְרָדְפֵהוּ.

Turn aside from the bad and do good; seek peace and pursue it.

Jewish tradition teaches that not only should we *seek* peace but we also should *pursue* peace in our homes, our communities, and the world. The mitzvah of pursuing peace is רְדִיפַת שָׁלוֹם.

How can treating others with respect add peace to your classroom community?

_____

How can avoiding gossip and rumors add peace to your school community?

_____

The mitzvah of pursuing peace in the home is שְׁלוֹם בַּיִת. What can you do to avoid family arguments?

Jewish tradition teaches that praying for peace does not by itself bring peace. But praying for our own willingness and ability to pursue peace can help us bring it about. בִּרְכַּת שָׁלוֹם focuses us on developing personal qualities, such as mercy and kindness, that can help us find שָׁלוֹם.

The seven בְּרָכוֹת of the עֲמִידָה on שַׁבָּת and holiday mornings are listed below.

1. אָבוֹת וְאִמָּהוֹת   2. גְבוּרוֹת   3. קְדוּשָׁה   4. קְדוּשַׁת הַיוֹם

5. עֲבוֹדָה   6. הוֹדָאָה   7. בִּרְכַּת שָׁלוֹם

Circle the name of the בְּרָכָה that can help focus us on the מִצְוָה of רְדִיפַת שָׁלוֹם.

 **Language Link**

Three words in בִּרְכַּת שָׁלוֹם remind us of parts of the body.

בְּעֵינֶיךָ is related to עֵינַיִם, meaning **eyes**. The singular form of עֵינַיִם is עַיִן.

פָּנֶיךָ is related to פָּנִים, meaning **face**.

But what is the third word that reminds us of a part of the body? It's בָּרוּךְ!

בָּרוּךְ shares a common root with the Hebrew word בֶּרֶךְ, meaning **knee**. בָּרוּךְ reminds us that blessing or praising God is like kneeling in front of a ruler. When we say a בְּרָכָה it is as if we are kneeling before God.

Here are the Hebrew names of several other parts of the body.

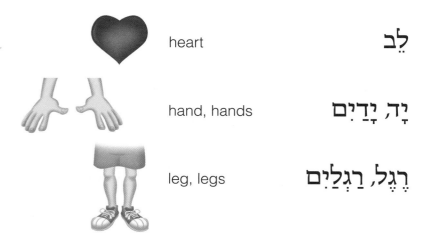

heart   לֵב

hand, hands   יָד, יָדַיִם

leg, legs   רֶגֶל, רַגְלַיִם

Handy Helpers

Write the Hebrew name for each body part described below.

1. We help carry your body when you pursue שָׁלוֹם. _____

2. I help you feel love and compassion when you recite prayers. _____

3. We help you see the good in people. _____

4. We help you reach out and share with those in need. _____

עֲשֵׂה שָׁלוֹם

The עֲשֵׂה שָׁלוֹם ("make peace") prayer is said immediately after the עֲמִידָה and asks God to make שָׁלוֹם in our lives and in the entire world.

Practice reading עֲשֵׂה שָׁלוֹם.

1. עֹשֶׂה שָׁלוֹם בִּמְרוֹמָיו, הוּא יַעֲשֶׂה שָׁלוֹם עָלֵינוּ,

2. וְעַל כָּל-יִשְׂרָאֵל (וְעַל כָּל-יוֹשְׁבֵי תֵבֵל). וְאִמְרוּ אָמֵן.

1. *May God who makes peace in the heavens, make peace for us*

2. *and for all Israel (and for all who live on the earth). And say, Amen.*

Prayer Variations

Some congregations include the phrase וְעַל כָּל-יוֹשְׁבֵי תֵבֵל "and for all who live on the earth" in the blessing for peace. Whether or not the phrase is included, we know that the prayer asks for peace for all the people of the world.

הוּא יַעֲשֶׂה שָׁלוֹם עָלֵינוּ

Prayer Words

Practice reading these words from the עֹשֶׂה שָׁלוֹם prayer.

makes	עֹשֶׂה
will make	יַעֲשֶׂה
for us, on us	עָלֵינוּ
and for, and on	וְעַל
all	כָּל
and say	וְאִמְרוּ
Amen	אָמֵן

P R A Y E R   P U Z Z L E

Complete the puzzle by writing the Hebrew word for each English word below.

Down

1. and say
2. all
3. makes
4. and for, and on

Across

1. Amen
3. for us, on us
4. will make

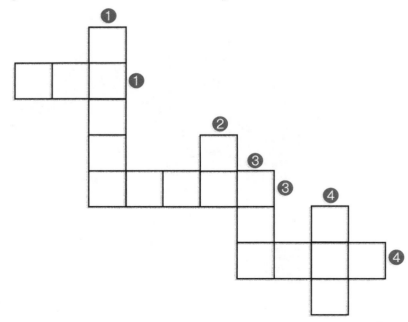

 At the Root

Words built on the root עלה have **go up** as part of their meaning.

Circle the root letters in each word below. (**Hint:** Remember that sometimes one of the root letters is missing from a word.)

וְיִתְעַלֶּה   עֲלִיָּה   עֶלְיוֹן   לַעֲלוֹת

The root of the four words above is _____ _____ _____.

Words built on this root have _____ as part of their meaning.

Which of the words above is the honor of being called up to the Torah? _____

 Moving to Israel, the holiest place in the world for the Jewish people, is called making עֲלִיָּה. Why do you think Judaism teaches that to settle in Israel *and* to be called to the Torah are to go up?

Going UP!

Start on the bottom step. Climb to the top by reading the words built on the root עלה. **Hint:** Sometimes only two root letters appear.

1. וְאָמְרוּ   לַעֲלוֹת   כָּל
2. יַעֲשֶׂה   חֶסֶד   עֶלְיוֹן
3. בְּעֵינֶיךָ   אָמֵן   עֲלִיָּה
4. עַמְּךָ   וְיִתְעַלֶּה   פָּנֶיךָ

How many words did you read? _____ Now go *down* the steps by reading *all* the words.

Jerusalem, City of Peace

According to legend, Jerusalem—יְרוּשָׁלַיִם—the capital of יִשְׂרָאֵל and the holiest city in all of יִשְׂרָאֵל, is named for שָׁלוֹם.

Circle the root letters that tell us that peace is part of Jerusalem's name: יְרוּשָׁלַיִם

Write your own blessing in English asking for שָׁלוֹם in יְרוּשָׁלַיִם.

בָּרוּךְ אַתָּה, יְיָ אֱלֹהֵינוּ, מֶלֶךְ הָעוֹלָם,

_____

Next year my family will be in Israel, where Batya and I will prepare for our bar and bat mitzvah celebration.

We will travel around Israel, study new prayers, and learn more about יְרוּשָׁלַיִם and peace. Please join us!

Until then, remember: Next year in Jerusalem—
לַשָׁנָה הַבָּאָה בִּירוּשָׁלַיִם

Clue to Cyberspace

שִׂים שָׁלוֹם are all prayers of peace. Read the "peace phrases" below. and,עֹשֶׂה שָׁלוֹם, שָׁלוֹם רָב

1. שָׁלוֹם רָב עַל יִשְׂרָאֵל עַמְּךָ

2. עֹשֶׂה שָׁלוֹם בִּמְרוֹמָיו

3. הוּא יַעֲשֶׂה שָׁלוֹם עָלֵינוּ

4. בְּכָל־עֵת וּבְכָל־שָׁעָה בִּשְׁלוֹמֶךָ

5. בָּרוּךְ אַתָּה, יְיָ, הַמְבָרֵךְ אֶת־עַמּוֹ יִשְׂרָאֵל בַּשָׁלוֹם

Which word in the lines above is the name of our Jewish homeland? _____

Use this clue to score bonus points in the "Balloon Float" game in Lesson 9— בִּרְכַּת שָׁלוֹם—on your computer.

מִלוֹן

א

אָבוֹת	fathers (patriarchs, ancestors)
אֲבוֹתֵינוּ	our fathers
אַבְרָהָם	Abraham
אֲדָמָה	earth
אוֹר	light
אֶחָד	one
אֲכִילַת	eating (of)
אֵל	God
אֱלֹהֵי	God of
אֱלֹהֵינוּ	our God
אִמָּהוֹת	mothers (matriarchs, ancestors)
אִמּוֹתֵינוּ	our mothers
אָמֵן	Amen
אֲנִי	I
אֵשׁ	fire
אַתָּה	you (for a boy or man)
אֶתְרוֹג	etrog

ב

(בְּ)אַהֲבָה	(in/with) love
בָּאֵלִם	among the gods (that other nations worship)
בְּדִבְרֵי	in the words of
בּוֹרֵא	who creates
בַּזְּמַן הַזֶּה	at this time
בְּחֶסֶד	with kindness
בֵּיתֶךָ	your house
בְּמִצְוֹתָיו	with God's commandments
בְּנֵי יִשְׂרָאֵל	Children of Israel
בַּסֻּכָּה	in the sukkah
בְּעֵינֶיךָ	in Your eyes
בַּעַל גְּבוּרוֹת	Powerful One
בְּקֹדֶשׁ	in holiness
בָּרוּךְ	blessed, praised
בְּרַחֲמִים	with compassion, mercy
בְּרָכָה, בְּרָכוֹת	blessing(s)
בְּרָכָה, בְּרָכוֹת שֶׁל מִצְוָה	blessing(s) when we do a mitzvah
בָּרְכוּ	bless! praise!
בִּרְכַּת הַמָּזוֹן	the blessing after a meal, Grace after Meals
בִּשְׁלוֹמֶךָ	with Your peace
בְּשָׂמִים	spices

ג

גִּבּוֹר	mighty, powerful
גְּבוּרוֹת	powers
גָּדְלֶךָ	Your greatness

ה

הָאֲדָמָה	the earth
הַבְדָּלָה	separation
הַגִּבּוֹר	the mighty
הַגָּדוֹל	the great
הַגֶּפֶן	the vine
הַזֶּה	this
הַזָּן	who feeds
הַכּוֹכָבִים	the stars
הַלַּיְלָה	the night
הַמְּאוֹרוֹת	the heavenly lights
הַמַּבְדִּיל	who separates
הַמְבָרֵךְ	who blesses
הַמְבֹרָךְ	who is to be blessed, praised
הַמּוֹצִיא	who brings forth
הָעוֹלָם	the world

ו

וְאָהַבְתָּ	you shall love
וְאַהֲבַת חֶסֶד	and a love of kindness
וְאִמְרוּ	and say
וּבוֹרֵא	and creates
(וּבְ)רָצוֹן	(and in/with) favor
וְהַנּוֹרָא	and the awesome
וָלַיְלָה	and night
וּמָגֵן	and shield
וּמוֹשִׁיעַ	and rescuer
וְעַל	and for, and on
וְצִוָּנוּ	and commands us
וְרַחֲמִים	and mercy

ז

זֵכֶר	memory
זִכָּרוֹן	memory

ח

חֹל	everyday
חַי	living, lives
חַיִּים	life
חֲנֻכָּה	Hanukkah
חֶסֶד	kindness
חֲסָדִים טוֹבִים	acts of loving-kindness
חֹשֶׁךְ	darkness

makes	עֹשֶׂה	

פ

wonder(s) — פֶּלֶא
Your face — פָּנֶיךָ
fruit(s) — פְּרִי, פֵּרוֹת

צ

Zion, Israel — צִיּוֹן

ק

holiness, Kiddush — קִדּוּשׁ
holiness — קְדוּשָׁה
holy — קֹדֶשׁ
makes us holy — קִדְּשָׁנוּ
sound, voice — קוֹל

ר

great — רַב
Rebecca — רִבְקָה
Rachel — רָחֵל

שׁ

shofar — שׁוֹפָר
grant, put — שִׂים
peace, hello, good-bye — שָׁלוֹם
peace in the home — שְׁלוֹם בַּיִת
your name, your name (to a boy or man) — שִׁמְךָ
hear — שְׁמַע
Sarah — שָׂרָה

ת

splendor, praises — תְּהִלַּת
Torah — תּוֹרָה
the Torah of life — תּוֹרַת חַיִּים

---

to affix — לִקְבֹּעַ
to hear — לִשְׁמֹעַ

מ

what [is] — מַה
thank, give thanks (boy/man) — מוֹדֶה
thank, give thanks (girl/woman) — מוֹדָה
mezuzah — מְזוּזָה
food — מָזוֹן
mezuzot — מְזוּזוֹת
gives life — מְחַיֶּה
who is like You — מִי כָמֹכָה
ruler, king — מֶלֶךְ
brings on the evening — מַעֲרִיב עֲרָבִים
matzah — מַצָּה
commandment(s) — מִצְוָה, מִצְוֹת
maror/bitter herbs — מָרוֹר

נ

Your prophet — נְבִיאֶךָ
miracles — נִסִּים
your soul — נַפְשְׁךָ
let us sanctify, make holy — נְקַדֵּשׁ
candle, light — נֵר

ע

helper — עוֹזֵר
supreme — עֶלְיוֹן
for us, on us — עָלֵינוּ
Your people — עַמְּךָ
tree — עֵץ
evening — עֶרֶב

ט

good — טוֹב
— טוֹ

יָדֶיךָ
לִי
will rule — יִמְלֹךְ
Jacob — יַעֲקֹב
will make — יַעֲשֶׂה
Isaac — יִצְחָק
Israel — יִשְׂרָאֵל

כ

God's glory — כְּבוֹדוֹ
as it is written — כַּכָּתוּב
all — כָּל/כָּל
all of us as one — כֻּלָּנוּ כְּאֶחָד

ל

Leah — לֵאָה
your heart — לְבָבְךָ
to bless — לְבָרֵךְ
from generation to generation — לְדוֹר וָדוֹר
lulav — לוּלָב
bread — לֶחֶם
(of the) going out from Egypt — (לִ)יצִיאַת מִצְרַיִם
(of the) work of creation — (לְ)מַעֲשֵׂה בְּרֵאשִׁית
forever and ever — לְעוֹלָם וָעֶד
to engage — לַעֲסוֹק